MW01181466

200
CROCHET
DESIGNS

HANNAH ELGIE & KATH WEBBER

SELLERS
PUBLISHING

A Quintet Book

Published by Sellers Publishing, Inc.
161 John Roberts Road, South Portland, Maine 04106
Visit our Web site: www.sellerspublishing.com
E-mail: rsp@rsvp.com

Copyright © 2017 Quintet Publishing Limited

All rights reserved. No part of this publication may be reproduced, stored
in a retrieval system, or transmitted in any form or by any means,
electronic, mechanical, photocopying, recording, or otherwise, without
the written permission of the copyright holder.

ISBN: 978-1-4162-4605-3
Library of Congress Control Number: 2016946051
QTT.THCB

This book was conceived, designed and produced by
Quintet Publishing Limited
Ovest House
58 West Street
Brighton
BN1 2RA

Project Editors: Julie Brooke, Leah Feltham
Photographer: Lydia Evans
Designers: Tania Field, Bonnie Bryan, Gareth Butterworth
Art Director: Michael Charles
Editorial Director: Emma Bastow
Publisher: Mark Searle
Pattern Consultants: Carol Meldrum, Carmel Searle

10 9 8 7 6 5 4 3 2 1

Printed in China by 1010 Printing

CONTENTS

introduction

This is the ultimate compendium for beginner, intermediate, and advanced crocheters. Use this guide as an introduction to the basics of the craft, and work through the designs to learn all the stitches you'll ever need to know, with a few professional hints and tips along the way.

The first thing to understand about crochet is that it can become an addiction — but let's face it, there are much worse addictions! Like its sister craft, knitting, crochet is satisfying, beautiful, and useful. With just a few simple and inexpensive tools (a hook, some yarn, a creative mind, and a little patience), you can create something wonderful from very little. Crochet lends itself to making dresses, afghans, and baby booties, as well as a variety of things for the home, such as doilies, coasters, and pot holders. It is a really versatile skill to have.

Crochet is a relatively new type of needlecraft, having only been popularized in the nineteenth century. "Crochet" comes from the French word for "hook," and with this single tool you can make any number of things. Combining a variety of stitches can result in hundreds of possibilities, and this book will teach you the basic techniques behind them. It also outlines 200 different crochet designs, taking you from beginner- right up to experienced-level designs, and gives you the skills to create some stunning crocheted items. Have fun!

how to use this book

Each pattern features four crochet designs and suggestions for how to use them. The main pattern teaches the basic techniques of the design, and then there are three variations offering alternatives to the main pattern and providing complementary designs to mix and match. The main skills you'll learn are as follows:

crocheting textured designs

Use crochet stitches to create textured fabric by working in circles and back and forth along a foundation chain. Additional interest is added using combinations of stitches, as well as by increasing and decreasing.

crocheting lace designs

Use this essential technique to make light and airy fabrics which really show off the stitches. By carefully spacing the stitches you can make simple yet intricate patterns.

crocheting shaped motifs

Using stars, circles, hearts, and other shapes that can be joined, you can make scarves, blankets, and decorative items. All the basic skills featured in this book can be applied to create the shaped designs in the final chapter. There is advice on using the shapes in projects, but see pages 14–15 for a more comprehensive guide to joining and finishing your work.

techniques and equipment

essential kit

Once you have chosen to start your crochet adventure, you'll need a few things to get you on your way. A local knitting or yarn store will almost certainly be able to get you started with some equipment for crocheting. Build a good relationship with them. They might even be able to suggest crochet social groups and outings, or even offer classes or workshops to improve your skills. If all else fails, there are hundreds, possibly thousands, of online craft stores that carry all the items you'll ever need.

You'll need the following items to get started:

Crochet hooks: These come in various sizes, from size 10 (1mm) for tiny and intricate lace work, up to large P/Q (15mm) and even size S or Z (19 or 35mm) hooks for super chunky yarn. We recommend starting with a size G (4mm) hook, for standard knitting yarn (called light worsted or double knitting). Alternatively, you can start with a larger hook and thicker yarn; this might help you to see the stitches more clearly. You'll need a size H (5mm) or size J (6mm) hook for worsted (aran) weight yarn, or a size L (8mm) hook for bulky (chunky) yarn.

Yarn: (see right).

Notions: These include **scissors** for cutting yarn, a large blunt **darning needle** for sewing in ends, and **stitch markers**.

Any other haberdashery items or embellishments in your sewing box can be used to adorn your work. These can include **buttons**, **beads**, and **sequins**.

a note about yarn

Once you have decided to learn to crochet, the fun part is choosing your yarn. Don't be restricted by what the pattern says; if you have seen some sumptuous yarn on sale, then go for it! All the designs in this book include a yarn suggestion, and that is the yarn used for the example. However, you need not be restricted to that yarn at all — you can substitute almost any yarn as long as you use the right size hook. If you're making a granny square and you want it thick and chunky, use a chunky weight yarn or wool. Or if you want tiny, delicate stitches, then use a 4-ply or lace weight yarn instead. You don't even need to use crochet cotton for your crochet; you can use any material. Even torn-up old sheets can be given a new lease on life with giant crochet hooks! To help you, here is a basic chart so you have the right tools for the job. Check the band on the yarn first for needle and hook size suggestions, but if you're not sure, then check below.

yarn weight	letter	hook size (metric)
4-ply (also known as fingering or sock yarn)	B	2.25 mm
light worsted/double knitting (also known as DK)	E/G	3.5 mm/4 mm
worsted (also known as aran)	H/I/J	5 mm/5.5 mm/6 mm
bulky (also known as chunky)	J/L	6 mm/8 mm
super bulky (also known as super chunky)	N/P	10 mm/12 mm
Hoopla yarn	L/M/N/O/P	8 mm/9 mm/10 mm/11 mm/12 mm

essential hints and tips

- When working in rows, you will always start with a foundation chain (see page 8).

- When working crochet stitches, you typically work each new stitch into the top of the stitches in the row below. If you look at the crochet from above, you'll see a series of "V"s that look like the chain. Insert the hook just under the "V," which will be working into the top 2 loops of the stitch. Working into just the front loop or just the back loop of the stitch will give you a ribbed, ridged effect, and the crocheted item will not lie flat.

- When working stitches in rows, you'll need to turn the work at the end of a row. Rotate your crochet from left to right 180 degrees, so that the hook is now on the right-hand side of the row.

- There is often a right side and wrong side in crochet. They look different, but can be equally attractive. When working in rows, alternate rows will be worked with the right side facing. In most patterns worked in the round, you'll be crocheting with the right side facing.

- When crocheting in rounds, you'll usually (though not always) begin with a foundation chain. Join the chain into a loop using a slip stitch: insert the hook into the very first chain made, yarn over hook (yoh) by bringing the working yarn from behind and over the hook, then pull this loop through the yarn on the hook. You will finish each round in the same way, inserting the hook into the first stitch worked, and drawing the yarn through the loop on the hook to slip stitch the ends together.

- Changing color is usually done at the end of the row, but can also be done mid-row. The technique is the same in both cases. Let the working yarn fall behind the work. Wrap the new color around the hook and pull a loop through the stitch on the hook. Pull the tail of the old color tight. You now have the new color as your working yarn. Tie the tails into a small tight knot behind the work to secure.

- To save time when working with more than one color, work in the ends as you go rather than weave them in at the end. When you change color, cut your tail ends the same length, then hold them along the top of the previous row. When you work the next row, you will work the stitches over the ends to conceal them.

how to crochet

Take time over these instructions, and remember that practice makes perfect. Use the hook in the hand that you write with but look at a mirror-image if you are left-handed. You can hold the hook like a pencil, or underneath your hand, however feels comfortable — there is no "right" or "wrong" way.

slip knot

To begin almost all crochet, you'll need to make a slip knot. You will need to have a fairly long bit of yarn ready. Make a loop with the yarn and pull the tail end (the end not attached to the ball of yarn) through and tighten. Pop that slip knot onto the crochet hook and tug sharply to pull it tight.

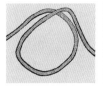 

holding the yarn

Once the slip knot is on the hook, hold your left hand out, palm up, or vice versa if you are left-handed. There are two ways of holding the yarn, shown below.

Slot the tail of the yarn between your pinkie and ring fingers and wrap it around the back of your hand. Point your index finger out and rest the yarn on your finger.

Another method of holding the working yarn is to wrap it twice around your index finger.

making a foundation chain

The foundation chain is the beginning of many of the designs in this book. Once done, it resembles a braid or a series of "V" shapes. Bring the hook under the yarn that rests on your index finger (1). Clasp the yarn around the hook (2) and pull it through the loop on the hook (3). Repeat this until you have the desired number of stitches (4). Count each stitch, but do not count the loop on your hook (5).

 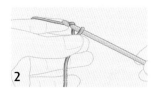

 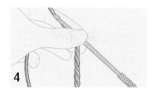

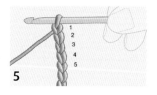

how to slip stitch

This stitch is used for joining, or working along to the next point in the pattern without forming part of the pattern. As you did for the foundation chain, insert the hook through the stitch and wrap the yarn over hook (yoh) by bringing your hook under the yarn resting on your finger and drawing it through the loop. You'll now have 2 loops on your hook. Draw the first one through the second one, leaving you with 1 loop on the hook.

single crochet

This small stitch is tight and neat, perfect for working with shaped motifs. One side of your foundation chain will have a series of little "V's".

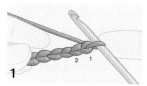

1 After you have made the foundation chain, count the chains back from the hook. Insert the hook into the second "V" along the hook.

2 Wrap the yarn around the hook and draw it back through this chain. You will now have 2 loops on the hook.

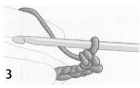

3 Wrap the yarn over the hook (yoh) again and draw it through both loops on the hook. You have made a single crochet! Continue into every chain until you get to the end of the foundation row.

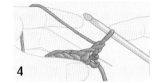

4 To work the next row, turn your work and make 1 chain stitch in the same way as for the foundation chain. This is the turning chain. Insert your hook into the first stitch under the top 2 loops and repeat steps 2 and 3. Repeat steps 2 and 3 across the row. Do not work into the turning chain of the previous row.

joining in a new color

Many of the designs in this book use more than one color.

1 Work the last stitch in the previous color but do not draw through the final yoh. You will have 2 loops on the hook.

2 Drop the old color behind your work and draw the new color through to complete the stitch. Continue working in the new color as indicated by the pattern.

double crochet

This is probably the most common crochet stitch, and produces a long, sturdy stitch perfect for making large blocks.

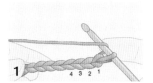

1 Yarn over and insert your hook into the fourth chain from your hook.

2 Yarn over and pull up a loop. You will have 3 loops on your hook.

3 Yarn over and draw through 2 loops. You will have 2 loops on your hook.

4 Yarn over and draw through 2 loops to complete the stitch. Yarn over, insert your hook into the next chain, and complete steps 2 to 4. Repeat into each chain across.

5 To work the next row, make 3 chain stitches in the same way as for the foundation chain. Turn your work. Insert your hook into the second stitch (skipping the first stitch because the chain 3 counts as a stitch.) Work under the top 2 loops and complete steps 2 to 4.

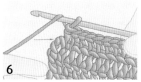

6 Continue working stitches into each stitch across the row. Your last stitch will be made into the top chain of the previous row's turning chain.

treble crochet

This is a long, loose stitch which crochets up quickly. Wrap the yarn around the hook twice, and then insert the hook into the stitch required. Wrap the yarn over the hook (yoh), pull the loop back through the stitch. There are now 4 loops on the hook. Yoh, pull through first 2 loops, yoh, pull through next 2 loops, yoh, and pull through final 2 loops on hook.

double treble crochet

This is very long and loose — it's not used frequently, but it is handy for creating height and lacy stitches. Wrap the yarn around the hook 3 times, and then insert the hook into the required stitch. Wrap the yarn over the hook (yoh), pull the loop back through the stitch. You now have 5 loops on the hook. Yoh, pull through first 2 loops, yoh, pull through next 2 loops, yoh, pull through next 2 loops, yoh pull through last 2 loops. For quadruple and quintuple treble crochet wrap the yarn around the hook 4 or 5 times as required.

turning chain

You will need to work extra chains at the beginning of each row or round for turning — how many will depend on which stitch you are using. The turning chain ensures there are enough stitches in the row overall, so add the following number of extra chains on your foundation to make sure you have enough stitches in the row:

For single crochet, 1 chain
For half double crochet, 2 chains
For double crochet, 3 chains
For treble crochet, 4 chains
For double treble, 5 chains

You will also work a turning chain at the beginning of each row. **This counts as the first stitch of your round or row.** Some crocheters find it simpler to work the turning chain before turning their work, but only do this when working back and forth along the foundation chain.

half double crochet

Wrap the yarn over the hook (yoh), insert hook into stitch. Yoh, draw loop through stitch so there are 3 loops on the hook. Yoh, draw yarn through all 3 loops on hook.

increasing

To increase the number of stitches in a row, simply work 2 or more stitches into 1 stitch in the previous row.

decreasing

To decrease stitches, you can skip a stitch and work over it into the next one. You can also crochet 2 stitches together on 1 row to create 1 stitch on the row above. This is normally a double crochet of 2 stitches together. Wrap the yarn over the hook (yoh), insert hook into stitch, yoh, draw yarn up through stitch. Yoh, draw through 2 loops on hook. Yoh, insert hook into the next stitch, yoh, draw yarn back up through the stitch. Yoh, pull yarn through 2 loops on hook, yoh, draw yarn through the 3 remaining loops on the hook. You are working the first part of the stitch into 1 stitch, then the first part of the stitch into the next stitch, then bringing them together. This will make a little upside-down "V" shape on your row. You can work 2 treble crochet stitches together in the same way.

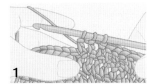
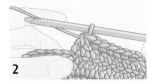

front post crochet

Insert the hook around the stitch on the row below from right to left, pushing the stitch to the front of the hook. Work stitch as usual.

back post crochet

Insert the hook around the stitch, from the back from right to left, pushing the stitch BEHIND the hook. Work the stitch as usual.

working in the round

As well as working a chain and joining it with a slip stitch, there are two other ways of making a circle:

Magic circles are ideal for closing tight centers. In this case, you simply wrap the tail of the yarn around your index finger, then tuck the end underneath as shown below in steps 1 and 2.

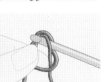

Hold the "magic circle" tightly between your thumb and forefinger on your yarn hand while you work the first few stitches for your foundation round. Join the round with a slip stitch and pull the yarn end tightly to close the circle.

Chain 2. Work the stitches into the second chain from the hook then join with a slip stitch. Pull the yarn end tightly to close the circle.

textural stitches

cluster stitch

You can work any number of stitches into the same original stitch (or "V") and create a cluster stitch. Typically, 3-double crochet stitches will be gathered together to form a cluster stitch. However, in this book there are examples of 2- and 4-double crochet cluster stitches and also 3-treble crochet cluster stitches.

To make a 3-double crochet cluster stitch:
Yoh, insert hook into stitch, yoh, draw yarn back up through stitch to get 3 loops on hook. Yoh, pull yarn through the first 2 loops on the hook, leaving 2 loops on hook. Yoh, insert hook back into the SAME stitch as before, yoh, and draw yarn back through the stitch. There are now 4 loops on the hook. Yoh, draw yarn through first 2 loops. Leaving 3 loops on the hook, yoh and insert hook back into the same original stitch again. Yoh, draw yarn through stitch, leaving 5 loops on the hook. Yoh, draw yarn through first 2 loops. Yoh once more, and draw this loop through the remaining loops on your hook. Essentially, you're working the first part of a double crochet (open double crochet), then starting over into the same stitch.

bobble stitch

Like a cluster stitch, work 4-open double crochet stitches into the same stitch: Yoh, insert hook into stitch, yoh, draw loop back through stitch, yoh, draw yarn through 2 loops on hook, leaving 5 loops on the hook. Yoh, draw through all 5 loops on hook. For an example, see page 22.

bullion stitch

Wrap the yarn around the hook 7 times (or as many times you like), then insert hook into the stitch. Yoh, draw the loop back through the stitch, then gently draw yarn through ALL loops on the hook. Work 1 chain stitch to secure. For an example, see page 24.

puff stitch

Again, you can work in any number of stitches to form a puff stitch, which is a very textural stitch. This instruction is for a typical puff stitch made of 3 half double crochets. Yoh, insert the hook into the required stitch, yoh, draw yarn back up through the stitch so there are 3 loops on the hook. Repeat this process 2 times, so there are 7 loops on the hook. Yoh, draw loop though all the remaining loops on the hook. Chain 1 stitch to "lock" or close the puff stitch. For an example, see page 62.

popcorn stitch

A popcorn stitch is a group of double crochet stitches folded together and closed at the top. The pattern will tell you to work a number of double crochet stitches into the required stitch. Remove the hook from the loop, leaving the loop relatively loose. Insert the hook into the top of the first double crochet of the group, and pick up the loop from the final double crochet of the group. Pull this loop through the loop on the hook to close the popcorn.

spike stitch

Spike stitches can be made in any stitch, but are usually made in single crochet. Insert the hook into the same stitch one or more rows below, yoh, draw the loop back through the stitch, yoh, draw through 2 loops on hook. For an example, see page 35.

extended single crochet

Insert hook into stitch, yoh, pull up 1 loop, and you'll have 2 loops on the hook. Yoh, pull through 1 loop. Yoh, pull through 2 loops. For an example, see page 44.

reading a pattern

The patterns in this book are written in abbreviations, all of which can be found in the chart below. Follow the instructions in the pattern, using this guide to work out which stitches to use.

full stitch name	abbreviation
back post double crochet/back post treble crochet	bpdc/bptr
beginning	beg
bobble stitch (make bobble)	mb
bullion stitch	bs
chains(s)	ch(s)
cluster stitch	cl
decrease	dec
double crochet	dc
double crochet 2 stitches together	dc2tog
double treble crochet	dtr
front post double crochet/front post treble crochet	fpdc/fptr
half double crochet	hdc
increase	inc
loops	lp(s)
previous	prev

full stitch name	abbreviation
puff stitch	ps
remaining	rem
repeat	rep
right side	rs
single crochet	sc
single crochet 2 stitches together	sc2tog
slip stitch	ss
skip (1 stitch)	sk
space	sp
spike stitch	sp st
treble crochet	tr
treble crochet 2 stitches together	tr2tog
turning chain	tch
wrong side	ws
yarn over hook	yoh

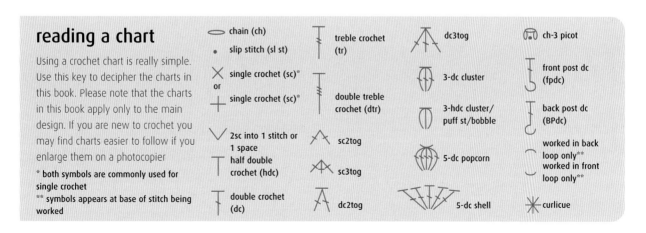

reading a chart

Using a crochet chart is really simple. Use this key to decipher the charts in this book. Please note that the charts in this book apply only to the main design. If you are new to crochet you may find charts easier to follow if you enlarge them on a photocopier

* both symbols are commonly used for single crochet
** symbols appears at base of stitch being worked

- chain (ch)
- slip stitch (sl st)
- single crochet (sc)* or
- single crochet (sc)*
- 2sc into 1 stitch or 1 space
- half double crochet (hdc)
- double crochet (dc)
- treble crochet (tr)
- double treble crochet (dtr)
- sc2tog
- sc3tog
- dc2tog
- dc3tog
- 3-dc cluster
- 3-hdc cluster/ puff st/bobble
- 5-dc popcorn
- 5-dc shell
- ch-3 picot
- front post dc (fpdc)
- back post dc (BPdc)
- worked in back loop only**
- worked in front loop only**
- curlicue

finishing your work

Finishing your work properly is often essential to the longevity and visual appeal of your crochet.

To fasten off your work, simply pull the loop that is on the hook nice and loose, and pass the working yarn through the loop, pulling tightly to make a neat knot. Fastening off in this way ensures an invisible join. Cut off the working yarn, leaving a tail of around 3 inches long.

To make the yarn ends disappear, you'll need to weave them into the work. Thread your darning needle, and pass the needle through the back of the stitches on the wrong side of the work, so you cannot see the weave from the front. Pass through as many stitches as you like to ensure an invisible end. Cut yarn if necessary.

blocking

"Blocking" is a term for shaping a crochet design. It's worth doing this to make the most of your work. The majority of designs in this book can, and should, be blocked. It doesn't take long and really ensures that the shape and construction of the work is shown as it should be. Some designs and fibers can simply be pulled into shape, but others will benefit from blocking — particularly shaped designs or those with curved edges (usually when a design is crocheted in single crochet).

For light blocking, lay the work out to its true shape and pin it. You can pin it to a folded towel or an ironing board. Place a damp cloth over the work and press lightly with a cool iron. Check the yarn label for care advice — some acrylic yarns should not be ironed.

For heavy blocking, usually with natural fibers, lay the work out and pin it. Saturate it with water (or starch for a stiff finish), using a spray bottle or something similar. Leave the work somewhere warm until totally dry. Remove the pins.

joining blocks

Joining blocks together is a great way of making projects, elevating crochet to much more than just the sum of its parts. The easiest way of joining blocks together is to use matching yarn and a darning needle.

First, lay out the blocks and decide which order they will go in. If you can, leave them on the floor or table in this order so that you can keep track, or take a photograph to refer back to if you're joining lots of blocks together. Work in rows, joining the top row together block by block. Once all the horizontal rows are joined together, you can join the vertical rows.

crocheting blocks together

slip stitch Match up the seams. Insert a crochet hook into a stitch on both blocks and pull the yarn back through. Slip this loop through the loop on the hook. Repeat into each stitch.

single crochet Match up the stitches, insert the hook into the first stitch, yoh, and pull back through stitches. Yoh, draw through both loops on hook. Repeat all the way along.

joining blocks "on-the-go"

This allows you to join crochet motifs as part of the final round of each one. Complete the first motif. Work the second motif to the end of the penultimate round. Ch1, insert hook from front to back into a stitch or space in the edge of the first motif at the point it should be joined to the second motif. Make a slip stitch and ch1 to complete the join. Continue to work the second motif until the next join. Ch1, insert hook from front to back into a stitch or space in the edge of the first motif. Make a slip stitch and ch1 to complete the join. Continue to work in this way until all the motifs have been worked and joined.

sewing blocks together

woven stitch Match the stitches on the blocks, and work the needle through them, passing the needle back and forth.

back stitch Match the stitches on both blocks, and work a back stitch seam for a firm join.

over stitch Match the stitches on both blocks, then work the needle around each stitch to join. For an almost invisible join, work through the back loop of the stitch.

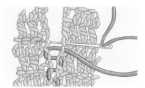

edgings

Blankets, scarves, and afghans all look beautiful with edgings. Here are some simple suggestions:

single crochet Using matching or contrasting yarn, work several rows/rounds of single crochet around the edge for a solid, simple edging.

picot edge Makes a simple, pretty edge. Chain 3, insert hook into the 3rd chain from the hook, yoh, draw through the stitch and the loop on the hook. Single crochet into the next stitch. Repeat picot, single crocheting along.

looped edge Chain 5, skip 5 stitches, single crochet into the next stitch.

shell edge Skip 2 stitches, work 5-double crochet into the next stitch, skip 2 stitches, work 1 single crochet into the next stitch.

granny edge Chain 3, work 2-double crochet stitches into the same stitch. Skip 2 stitches, work 3-double crochet into the next, repeat, work 3-double crochet, chain 3, then 3-double crochet into the corners.

fringe Fringing is very simple. Cut 4 pieces of yarn of equal lengths. Fold all 4 pieces in half, insert the hook into the stitch, and grab the fold with the hook. Draw a loop through the stitch. Place the cut ends through the loop and pull to tighten.

Texture

These designs provide plenty of visual interest thanks to the way the different stitches used in them are grouped in rows and clusters.

flat circles

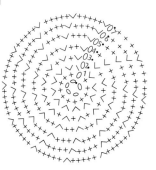

Materials

size G hook

King Cole Bamboo Cotton DK in Rose (A), Opal (B), Plum (C)

circular pillow pad for project

Project notes

Pillow. Work 2 pieces in single crochet, working single row color stripe sequence as follows: work Round 1 in yarn A, Round 2 in yarn B, Round 3 in yarn C, repeat stripe to end to match the cushion pad size. Sew the circles halfway together, insert the pad and sew around the rest of the outer edge.

Main pattern: using yarn A, ch5, join with ss to form a ring.

Round 1: ch1 (does not count as a sc throughout), 12sc into ring, join with ss into first sc. [12 sc]

Round 2: ch1, * 2sc into each st around, join with ss into first sc. [24 sc]

Round 3: ch1, * work 2sc into next st, work 1sc into next st **, rep from * to ** 11 times more, join with ss into first sc. [36 sc]

Round 4: ch1, * work 2sc into next st, work 1sc into each of next 2sts **, rep from * to ** 11 times more, join with ss into first sc. [48 sc]

Round 5: ch1, * work 2sc into next st, work 1sc into each of next 3sts ** rep from * to ** 11 times more, join with ss into first sc. [60 sts]

Round 6: ch1, * work 2sc into next st, work 1sc into each of next 4sts **, rep from * to ** 11 times more, join with ss into fist sc. [72 sts]

Round 7: ch1, * work 2sc into next st, work 1sc into each of next 5 sts **, rep from * to ** 11 times more, join with ss to first sc. [84 sc] Fasten off, weave in ends.

NOW TRY THIS

Half double crochet

Using yarn A, work as given for main pattern, using hdc and ch2 at beginning of each round throughout.

Double crochet

Using yarn B, work as given for main pattern, using dc and ch3 at beg of each round throughout.

Treble crochet

Using yarn C, work as given for main pattern, using tr and ch4 at beg of each round throughout.

box

Materials

size G hook

Rowan Wool Cotton DK in Coffee (A), Inky (B), Elf (C), Antique (D)

Project notes

Pot holder. Crochet 2 blocks of main pattern. With wrong sides facing, sc together with contrasting yarn. Make a hanging loop by making a rectangle (see Rectangles, page 77) and insert it into the corner of the piece. Make a pretty, loopy edge by working * ch5, sc into next stitch. Repeat from * around the pot holder.

Main pattern: using yarn D, ch6.

Row 1: 1dc into 4th ch from hook, 1dc each into each of next 2ch, turn. Break off yarn D and join in yarn A.

Row 2: ch6, 1dc into 4th ch from hook, 1dc into each of next 2ch, sk2, ss into top of ch3 of the first square, ch3, work 2dc around stem of st and 1dc into 1st ch, turn. Break off yarn A and join in yarn B.

Row 3 (increasing): ch6, 1dc into 4th ch from hook and into each of next 2ch, * sk3, ss into top of next ch3, work 3dc around stem of next st *. Break off yarn B and join in yarn C.

Rows 4–9: Keeping stripe sequence correct, repeat last row 6 more times. See images for stripe sequence.

Row 10 (decreasing): ss into next 3sts and top of ch3, * ch3, 1dc into ch3 of prev row, sk3, ss into top of next ch3, rep from * to end, turn. Repeat last row, while maintaining stripe sequence, until a square is formed. Fasten off and weave in ends

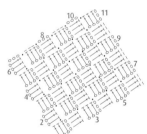

Block stripe

Work as given for main pattern, with 2 rows of each color for a bold stripe effect, working 6 increase rows before switching to decrease rows to form a square.

Broken boxes

Work as for the main pattern, in yarn D. Do not turn. Using yarn C for a contrasting color, work a row of sc in contrasting yarn between each "box" row, using 3sc for the outer corners for each "box" and ss into the inner corner. Work sc row with rs facing, then turn to work next "box" row.

Stripes

Using yarn C, ch20+3.

Row 1: 3dc into 4th ch from hook, * sk3, work (1sc, ch3, 3dc) into next st, rep from * to end, working 1sc into last st. Change to yarn A. **Row 2:** ch3, turn, 3dc into first sc of row below. * 1sc, ch3, 3dc into 3ch, rep from * to end, 1sc into last st, turn. Row 2 forms the pattern. Repeat.

solid weave

Materials

size G hook

Debbie Bliss Cotton DK in Aqua (A), Apple Green (B), Pigeon (C), Earth (D)

Main pattern: Using yarn A, ch21.
Row 1: 1sc into 2nd ch from hook, 1sc into each ch to end, turn (20sts).
Row 2: ch1, 1sc into first st, 1sc into each st to end.
Repeat Row 2 a further 22 times. Fasten off and weave in ends.

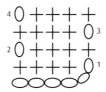

NOW TRY THIS

Double crochet

Using yarn B, ch23.
Row 1: 1dc into 4th ch from hook, 1dc into each ch to end, turn (20sts). **Row 2:** ch3, 1dc into first st, 1dc into each st to end, turn. Repeat Row 2 another 11 times.

Half double crochet

Using yarn C, ch22.
Row1: 1hdc into 3rd ch from hook, 1hdc into each ch to end, turn (20sts). **Row 2:** ch2, 1hdc into first st, 1hdc into each st to end, turn. Repeat Row 2 a further 16 times.

Treble crochet

Using yarn D, ch25.
Row 1: 1tr into 5th ch from hook, 1 tr into each ch to end (20sts). **Row 2:** ch5, 1tr into first st, 1tr into each st to end, turn. Repeat Row 2 a further 7 times.

shelley

Materials

size G hook

Sublime Baby Cashmere Merino
Silk DK in Button (A), Teddy (B), Raffia (C)

wooden beads: Beaded variation

Main pattern: Multiple of 6+7 (add 3 for turning ch). Using yarn A, ch28.

Row 1: 2dc into 4th ch from hook, * sk2ch, 1sc into next ch, sk2ch, 5dc into next ch, sk2ch, 1sc into next ch, rep from * ending with 3dc into last ch, turn.

Row 2: ch1, 1sc into first dc, sk2, 5dc into first sc of previous row, * sk2, 1sc into next st (center st of 5dc), sk2, 5dc into next st, rep from * ending last rep with sc into top of tch, turn.

Row 3: ch3, 2dc into 1st st, * sk2, 1sc into next st (center of 5dc), sk2, 5dc into next st, rep from * ending last rep with 3dc into last sc, turn.

Rows 2–3 form the pattern; repeat to required length. Fasten off and weave in ends.

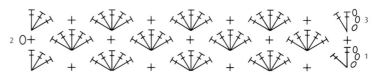

NOW TRY THIS

Wavy

Work as given for main pattern, using yarn A for Row 1 and yarn B for Row 2, keeping stripe sequence as set throughout.

Beaded

Work as given for main pattern using yarn B. Thread beads onto your yarn before starting and add in the beads as you crochet.

Diagonal stripes

Work as given for main pattern using yarn B and yarn C as follows. **Row 1:** work as main pattern. **Row 2:** 1st full shell in yarn C. **Row 3:** 3rd full shell in yarn C. **Row 4:** 2nd full shell in yarn C. **Row 5:** 2nd full shell in yarn C. Keeping pattern as set, moving colored shell over 1 each row.

bob

Materials

size G hook

King Cole Bamboo Cotton DK in
Aqua (A), Yellow (B), Rose (C),
Moss (D), Plum (E)

Notes

MB=make bobble. To make a bobble, work 4
open dc in same st leaving 5 loops on hook,
draw yarn through all 5 loops.

Main pattern: using yarn A, ch23.

Row 1: 1sc into 2nd ch from hook, 1sc into each ch to end, turn (22sts).

Rows 2-4: ch1, 1sc into each st to end, turn.

Row 5: ch1, 1sc into each of next 3sts, *MB, 1sc into each of next 4sts, rep from * 3 more times, 1sc into each of next 3sts.

Rows 2–5 form the bobble pattern. Repeat these rows until 4 sets of bobbles have been completed. Then repeat Rows 2–4 once more. Fasten off and weave in ends.

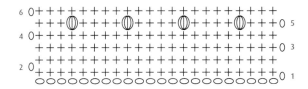

NOW TRY THIS

Multicolored bobbles

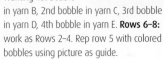

Using yarn A, work Rows 1–5 as given for main pattern, working 1st bobble in yarn B, 2nd bobble in yarn C, 3rd bobble in yarn D, 4th bobble in yarn E. **Rows 6–8:** work as Rows 2–4. Rep row 5 with colored bobbles using picture as guide.

Alternate bobbles

Using yarn D, work Rows 1–5 as given for main pattern, working all bobbles in yarn C.
Rows 6–8: work as Rows 2–4. **Row 9:** ch1, 1sc into next 6 sts, * MB, 1sc into each of next 4 sts, rep from * twice more, 1sc into last st, turn. Repeat from Row 2 until 5 sets of bobbles have been worked. Work Rows 2–4.

Striped bobbles

Work as given for main pattern, working Rows 1–4 in yarn E, and Row 5 in yarn B, alternating between colors using the picture as a guide.

bullion

Materials

size G hook

Debbie Bliss Cotton DK in
Purple (A), Teal Blue (B)

Notes

BS=bullion stitch. Wrap the yarn 7 times
around the hook, insert the hook into the
next ch sp, pull through a loop, wrap the yarn
again, and pull through all the loops on the
hook.

Main pattern: using yarn A, ch17.

Row 1: 1sc into 2nd ch from hook, 1sc into each ch to end, turn.

Row 2: ch3, sk1, 1dc into each of next 4sts, * 1BS in next st, 1dc into each of next 5sts,
rep from * to end, working last dc into top of tch, turn.

Row 3: ch1, sk1, 1sc into each st to end, 1sc into top of tch, turn.

Row 4: ch3, sk1, 1dc into next st, * 1BS into next st, 1dc into each of next 5sts, rep
from * to last 3 sts, 1BS into next st, 1dc into next st, work last dc into top of tch, turn.

Row 5: work as Row 3.

Row 6: work as Row 2.

Row 7: work as Row 3.

Row 8: work as Row 4.

Row 9: work as Row 3.

Row 10: work as Row 2.

Row 11: work as Row 3. Fasten off and weave in ends.

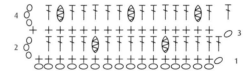

NOW TRY THIS

Color stripe

Work as given for main
pattern, working every
odd row in yarn A and
every even row in yarn
B. Continue working in
stripes as set.

Bullion in a different color

Work as given for main
pattern, working every
bullion st in yarn B.

Full-on bullion

Using yarn B, work as
follows: **Row 1:** work
as Row 1 in main
pattern. **Row 2:**
ch3, sk1, work 1BS into
every st to end, 1BS into top of tch, turn.
Row 3: ch1, sk1, 1sc into each st to
end, 1sc into top of tch turn. Rows 2–3
form the pattern. Repeat until 9 rows
have been worked.

knot

Materials

size G hook

Sublime Baby Cashmere Merino DK in
Gray (A), Pink (B)

Main pattern: using yarn A, ch12.
Row 1: 1sc into 2nd ch from hook, 1sc into each ch to end, turn.
Row 2: ch1, 1sc into next st, * 1tr into next st, 1sc into next st, rep from * to end, turn.
Row 3: ch1, 1sc into each st to end, turn.
Rows 2–3 form the pattern. Repeat for a further 9 rows. Fasten off and weave in ends.

NOW TRY THIS

Offset knot

Using yarn B, ch12.
Rows 1–3: work as given for main pattern. **Row 4:** ch1, 1sc into each of next 2sts, * 1tr into next st, 1sc into next st, rep from * to last 2sts, 1sc into last 2sts, turn. **Row 5:** work as Row 3. Rows 2–5 form the pattern; repeat to required length.

Two-color knot

Work as given for Offset knot, but work odd rows in yarn A and even rows in yarn B.

Dense knot

Using yarn A, work as for Offset knot but omitting sc rows.

beachcombing

Materials

size J hook: main, Target and Shell

size G hook: Spiral granny square

Drops Karisma DK in Rust (A), Green (B), Sublime Chunky Merino Tweed in Forage (C)

King Cole Smooth DK in Pewter (D), Spearmint (E), Cobalt (F), Rose (G)

stitch marker

Main pattern: Using yarn A, ch4, join with ss to form a ring.

Round 1: ch1 (counts as 1st sc), 13sc into ring, do not join. Place stitch marker into first st of round.

Round 2: 2sc into each st to end. Move stitch marker to 1st st of next and every following round.

Round 3: * 1sc into each of next 2sts, 2sc into next st, rep from * to end.

Round 4: * 1sc into each of next 3sts, 2sc into next st, rep from * to end.

Round 5: * 1sc into each of next 4 sts, 2sc into next st, rep from * to end.

Round 6: * 1sc into each of next 5sts, 2sc into next st, rep from * to end. Fasten off and weave in ends.

NOW TRY THIS

Shell

Using yarn C, ch4, join with ss to form a ring.

Round 1: 8sc into ring, do not join with ss, work (2hdc into back loop of next st) 5 times, (2dc into back loop of next st) 9 times, (2tr into back loop of next st) 7 times, (1tr into back loop of next st, 2tr into back loop of next st) 7 times, 1tr into back loop of next st, 2tr into back loop of next st, 2tr into back loop of next st. Fasten off.

Spiral granny square

Using yarn A, make a magic loop. **Round 1:** * ch1 (does not count as sc), 1sc, 1hdc, 2dc** into magic loop. Drop yarn A behind, leaving a long loop to avoid pulling the stitch, but leaving the stitch live. Pick up yarn B through magic loop. Repeat from * to ** with yarns B, C, and D. Do not fasten off. Pull tail of yarn A to close magic loop. **Round 2:** Continuing with yarn D, *(2dc into first st, 1dc into next st) twice.** Repeat from * to ** with yarns A, B and C. **Round 3:** Continuing with yarn C, * (ch2,

1dc into next st, sk 1, 2dc into each of next 2 sts, sk 1, 1dc into last st) **. Repeat from * to ** with yarns D, A and B. **Round 4:** Continuing with yarn D, *(2dc, ch2, 2dc) into ch sp, sk 1, (3dc, sk 1) 3 times **. Repeat from * to ** with yarns A, B and C. **Round 5:** Continuing with yarn A, (3dc, ch1, 3dc) into ch sp, sk 2, (1hdc, 1sc, 1ss) into next st.

Target

Work as given for main pattern, working Rounds 1, 3, and 5 in yarn A and Rounds 2, 4 and 6 in yarn B.

waffle

Materials

size G hook

Sublime Baby Cashmere Merino Silk DK
in Baby Pink (A), Beige (B), Green (C)

Main pattern: Using yarn A, ch21.

Row 1: 1dc into 4th ch from hook, 1dc into each ch to end, turn.

Row 2: ch3, * work 1dc around front post of next 2sts (fpdc), work 1dc into next st, rep from * to end, turn.

Row 3: ch3, 1dc into each of next 2sts, * 1fpdc into next st, 1dc into each of next 2sts, rep from * to end, 1fpdc in last st, turn.

Rows 2–3 form pattern; repeat these rows until 11 rows have been worked. Fasten off and weave in ends.

Bumpy
Work as given for main pattern, alternating between A and B yarns.

Texture
Using yarn C, ch22. Work as for the main pattern, using tr throughout and ch4 for turning chain.

Double waffle
Using yarn C, ch22.
Row 1: 1dc into 4th ch from hook, 1dc into each ch to end, turn. **Row 2:** ch3, sk 1st st, 1dc into next st, * 1fpdc into each of next 2sts, 1dc into each of next 2sts, rep from * ending last rep with 1dc into last st, turn. Row 2 forms the pattern. Repeat until 13 rows are worked.

tweedy square

Materials

size G hook

Debbie Bliss Cotton DK in Brown (A), Beige (B), Grass Green (C), Light Turquoise (D)

Main pattern: using yarn A, ch26.

Row 1: 1sc into 2nd ch from hook, 1sc into each ch to end, turn.

Row 2: ch1, 1sc into 1st st, * ch2, sk2, 1sc into next st, repeat from * to end, turn.

Row 3: ch3, 1dc into 1st st, * sk2, 3dc into next st, repeat from * ending last rep with 2dc, turn.

Rows 2–3 form the pattern; repeat until 16 rows have been worked. Fasten off and weave in ends.

NOW TRY THIS

Mixed stripes

Work as given for main pattern, working Rows 1–6 in yarn B, Row 7 in yarn A, Row 8 in yarn B, and Row 9 in yarn A. Rows 1–9 form stripe sequence while keeping pattern. Repeat stripe to required length.

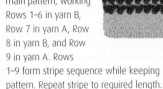

Single row stripe

Work as given for main pattern, alternating rows between yarn C and yarn D.

Half double crochet

Using yarn D, work as given for main pattern using hdc throughout and ch3 for turning.

curlicues

Materials

size G hook

Sublime Baby Cashmere Merino Silk DK in Ragdoll (A), Piglet (B), Puzzle (C), Cuddle (D)

Main pattern: using yarn A, ch17.

Row 1: 1dc into 4th ch from hook, 1dc into each ch to end, turn.

Row 2: ch3, 1dc into each st to end, turn.

Row 3: ch3, 1dc into each of next 4sts, * ch10, 2dc into 4th ch from hook, 3dc into each of next ch6 (1st curlicues worked), ss in top of last dc worked in main fabric, 1dc into each of next 5sts, rep from * to end, turn.

Row 4: repeat Row 2.

Row 5: ch3, 1dc into each of next 2sts, * ch10, 2dc into 4th ch from hook, 3dc into each of next 6sts, ss in top of last dc worked in main fabric, 1dc into each of next 5sts, rep from * to end, omitting last 3dc of final rep, turn.

Rows 6–9: Repeat Rows 2–5 once more to set the pattern.

Row 10: ch3, 1dc into each st across. Fasten off, weave in ends.

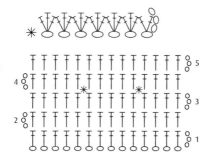

NOW TRY THIS

Color variation

Work as given for main pattern using yarn B for curlicues.

Little curlicues

Using yarn C, work as given for main pattern, working each curlicue as follows: ch6, 2sc in 2nd ch from hook, 3sc in each of next ch4.

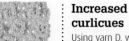

Increased curlicues

Using yarn D, work as given for main pattern, working each curlicue as follows: ch6, 3sc in 2nd ch from hook, 3hdc in next st, 3dc in next st, 3tr in next st, 3dtr in last st.

candy

Materials

size H hook

Rowan All Seasons Cotton in
241 Damson (A), 242 Blush (B),
246 Hedge (C), 239 Jacuzzi (D)

Main Pattern: using yarn A, ch2.

Row 1: 3sc into 2nd ch from hook, turn.

Row 2: ch1, 1sc into each of 1st 2sts, 2sc into last st, turn.

Row 3: ch1, 1sc into each of 1st 3sts, 2sc into last st, turn. Fasten off yarn A and join in yarn B.

Row 4: ch1, 1sc into each st to last st, 2sc into last st.
Repeat Row 4 until there are 20 sts, changing color every 3rd row.

Next row: ch1, 1sc into each st to end, turn.

Next row (dec): ch1, sk1, 1sc into each st to last st, sk1, 1sc into ch1.
Repeat last row until 2 sts remain.

Next row: ch1, sc2tog. Fasten off and weave in ends.

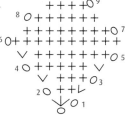

NOW TRY THIS

Single color stripes

Work as given for main pattern, working each row in a different color yarn. Rows 1 and 3 in yarn A, Rows 4 and 7 in yarn B, and Rows 8 and 12 in yarn C. Work the remaining increase rows in yarn A, and then reverse the stripe for decrease rows.

Block stripes

Work as given for main pattern, working increase rows in yarn B and C in a 2-row stripe, then change to yarn D for decrease rows.

Double crochet diagonal stripes

Work pattern as given below, changing colors every 2 rows. **Row 1:** ch4, 2dc into 4th ch from hook, turn. **Row 2:** ch3, 2dc into 1st st, 1dc into next, 3dc into last st, turn. **Row 3:** ch3, 2dc into 1st st, 1dc into each st until last st, 3dc into last st. Repeat Row 3 until there are 20sts. **Next row:** ch3, 1dc into each st to end. **Next row (dec):** ch3, sk1, dc2tog, 1dc into each st to last 3 sts, sk1, dc2tog. Repeat last row until 2 sts, dc2tog. Fasten off.

spiked

Materials

size G hook

Sublime Baby Cashmere Merino Silk DK in Teddy Red (A), Caterpillar (B), Seesaw (C), Ragdoll (D)

Main pattern: using yarn A, ch18+1 for turning.

Row 1: 1sc into 2nd ch from hook, 1sc into each ch to end, turn.

Rows 2–3: ch1, 1sc into each st to end, turn. Fasten off yarn A and join in yarn B.

Row 4: ch1, 1sc into 1st st, * work 1 spike st (by inserting hook 1 row below and working sc as normal * 1sc into next st, rep from * to end, turn.)

Row 5: work as Row 2. Break off yarn B and join in yarn A.

Row 6: work as Row 4.

Rows 7–9: work as Rows 1–3. Repeat Rows 1–9 to set pattern. Fasten off and weave in ends.

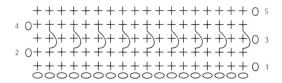

NOW TRY THIS

Bird's foot clusters

Using yarn C, ch18+1 and work Rows 1–3 as given for main pattern. Fasten off yarn C and join in yarn B. **Row 4:** ch1, 1sc into each of next 2sts, * work bird's foot cluster (BFC) as follows: Insert hook into stitch to right of st below, yarn over, pull loop through, insert hook into st below on row below, yoh, pull loop through, insert hook into st to left of st on row below, yoh, pull loop through, yoh, pull loop through all loops on hook to close cluster, 1sc into next 3sts, rep from * to

end. **Rows 5–7:** work as Rows 2–3. **Row 8:** work as Row 4, working BFC on right-side facing rows.

Rake stitch

Using yarn D, ch17 and work Rows 1–3 as given for main pattern. Fasten off yarn D and join in yarn C. **Row 4:** work 1 spike st into next 5 sts 3 rows below, 1dc into next 5 sts, 1 spike st into next 5 sts 3 rows below, turn. **Rows 5–6:** work as Rows 2–3. Repeat Rows 1–6.

Eyelash spike stitch

Using yarn C, ch18+1 and work Rows 1–3 as given for main pattern. Fasten off yarn C and join in yarn A. **Row 4:** ch1, 1sc into 1st st, * 1 spike st on row below, 1 spike st on 2 rows below, 1 spike st on 3 rows below, 1 spike st on 2 rows below, 1 spike st on 1 row below, 1sc into next st, rep from * twice more, 1sc into last st, turn. **Rows 5–7:** work as Rows 1–3. Repeat Rows 4–7.

fruit punch

Materials

size G hook

King Cole Bamboo Cotton DK in Yellow (A), Moss (B), Oyster (C), Damson (D)

Note

When making the pineapples make the loops longer than usual to make it easier to pull the yarn through 8 loops to complete the stitch.

Main pattern: using yarn A, ch15+3 for turning ch.

Row 1: work into 4th ch from hook as follows: * (yoh, draw loop through ch leaving loops on hook) 4 times, yoh and draw through 8 loops, yoh and draw through 2 loops (1 pineapple made), ch1, sk1, rep from * ending last rep with 1dc into last ch.

Row 2: ch3, 1 pineapple into 1st ch sp,* ch1, 1 pineapple into next ch sp, rep from * to end, 1dc into tch, turn.

Row 2 forms the pattern; repeat to required length. Fasten off and weave in ends.

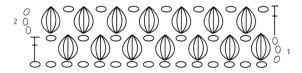

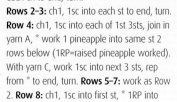

NOW TRY THIS

Raised pineapples

Using yarn C, ch20.

Row 1: 1sc into 2nd ch from hook, 1sc into each ch to end, turn.

Rows 2–3: ch1, 1sc into each st to end, turn.

Row 4: ch1, 1sc into each of 1st 3sts, join in yarn A, * work 1 pineapple into same st 2 rows below (1RP=raised pineapple worked). With yarn C, work 1sc into next 3 sts, rep from * to end, turn. **Rows 5–7:** work as Row 2. **Row 8:** ch1, 1sc into first st, * 1RP into next st, 1sc into next 3sts, rep from * 3 more times, 1RP into next st, 1sc into last st, turn. Rows 2–8 form the pattern. Repeat once more, then Rows 2–3. Fasten off.

Pineapples with leaves

Work alternate rows in yarns A and B for a leafy pineapple effect, using the picture as a guide.

Blackberries

Ch18. Using yarn C, work Rows 1–3 as given for Raised pineapples. Work Row 4 as given for main pattern, using yarn D to make blackberries. Work Row 5 as Row 2 using yarn B. Continue with pattern, working 7 rows of sc between blackberry rows.

solid granny square

Materials

size G hook

King Cole Bamboo Cotton DK in
Moss (A), Yellow (B),
Aqua (C), Plum (D)

Main pattern: using yarn A, ch5, join with ss to form a ring.

Round 1: ch3 (counts as 1dc), 2dc into ring, * ch3 (1st corner worked), 3dc into ring, rep from * twice more, ch3, join with ss into top of ch3 at beg of round.

Round 2: ch3 (counts as 1dc),* work 1dc into each st to corner, (3dc, ch3, 3dc) into corner sp, rep from * and join with ss into top of ch3 at beg of round.

Rounds 3–5: work as for Row 2. Fasten off and weave in ends.

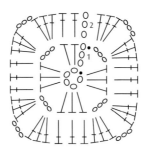

NOW TRY THIS

Maze

Work as given for main pattern for Rounds 1, 3, and 5 using yarn C. Work Rounds 2 and 4 using yarn D. **Round 2:** ch3 (counts as 1dc), 2dc, 2ch, 3dc into 1st ch2sp, * ch1, 3dc, 2ch, 3dc into next ch2sp, rep from * twice more, ch1, join with ss into top of ch3, turn. **Round 4:** Join in yarn C into corner ch2sp, ch3 (counts as 1dc), (2dc, ch2, 3dc) into ch2sp, (*sk2, 3dc into next st, ch1**, rep from * to ** twice more, (3dc, 2ch, 3dc) into next corner st) twice, then repeat from * to ** three times, join with ss to ch3.

Color changing rounds

Work as given for main pattern. Rounds 1, 3, and 5, work in yarn A. For Rounds 2 and 4, work in yarn B.

Treble crochet

Using yarn B, work as given for main pattern, but use tr throughout, working ch4 at the beg of each round and ch4 for corner spaces.

ripples and waves

Materials

size G hook

Sublime Baby Cashmere Merino DK in
Splash (A), Marmite (B),
Vanilla (C), Ragdoll (D)

Main pattern: Multiple of 14 + 3 for turning ch. Using yarn A, ch28+3.

Row 1: 1dc into 4th ch from hook, 1dc into each of next 4ch, * (dc2tog) twice (decrease worked), 1dc into each of next 4ch, (2dc into next ch) twice (increase worked), 1dc into each of next 4ch, rep from * ending last rep with 2dc into last ch, turn.

Row 2: ch3 (counts as 1dc), 1dc into base of ch3, 1dc into each of next 4sts, * (dc2tog) twice (decrease worked), 1dc into each of next 4sts, (2dc into next st) twice (increase worked), 1dc into each of next 4st, rep from * ending last rep after 1st set of 2dc into next st, turn.

Row 2 forms pattern; repeat to required length. Fasten off and weave in ends.

NOW TRY THIS

Raspberry ripple

Using yarn A, work as given for main pattern, changing to yarn D at the end of the row for stripe. Alternate rows of yarns A and D for pattern.

Single crochet

Using yarns B and C, work as given for Raspberry ripple, working in sc throughout and using ch1 for turning.

Ribbed effect

Using yarn D, work as given for main pattern for Row 1, then for Row 2, work as for the main pattern but working into the back loop of each st.

cornered

Materials

size H hook

Rowan All Seasons Cotton in Jacuzzi (A), Damson (B), Blush (C), Hedge (D)

Main pattern: using yarn A, ch4, join with ss to form a ring.

Row 1: ch3 (counts as 1st st), (2hdc, ch3, 3hdc) into ring, turn.

Row 2: ch3, sk1, 1dc into each of next 2sts, (2dc, ch3, 2dc) into ch3sp, 1dc into each of next 3sts, turn.

Row 3: ch3, sk1, 1dc into each st to ch3sp, (3dc, ch3, 3dc) into ch3sp, 1dc into each st to end, turn.

Row 3 forms pattern; repeat to required length. Fasten off and weave in ends.

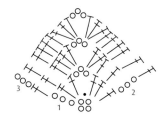

NOW TRY THIS

Striped corner square

Work as given for main pattern, working Rows 1–2 in yarn B and Row 3 in yarn C. Keeping pattern correct, work in stripe sequence using the picture as a guide.

Single crochet

Using yarn B, ch4, join with ss to form a ring. **Row 1:** ch1, 3sc, 1hdc, 3sc into ring, turn. **Row 2:** ch1, 1sc into each sc, work (1sc, 1hdc, 1sc) into next st (corner worked), 1sc into each st to end, turn. **Row 3:** ch1, sk1, 1sc into each sc, work (1sc, 1hdc, 1sc) into next st (corner worked), 1sc into each sc to end, turn. Repeat last row to required size.

Treble crochet

Using yarn D, work as given for main pattern, with ch4 for turning, change each dc to tr and work ch4 for corner ch sp.

spinning wheels

Materials

size G hook

Araucania Chacabuco (A)

Sublime Baby Cashmere Merino Silk DK in Cheeky (B), Caterpillar (C), Piglet (D), Puffin (E)

Project notes

Potholder. Using a size H hook and a color-changing yarn (such as Araucania Chacabuco), work the main pattern. Fasten off. Make a strap as follows: ch8, turn, work 1dc into 4th ch from hook, and 1 dc into each ch to end, turn. * Ch3, sk1, 1dc into each st to end, turn. Rep from * until strap is of desired length. Fasten off, fold strap in half, and stitch to corner of block using a tapestry needle.

Main pattern: using yarn A, ch6, join with ss to form a ring.

Round 1: * ch5, 4tr cl into ring, ch5, ss to ring (1st cluster worked), rep from * 3 more times, join with ss into base of ch5.

Round 2: * ch2, 12tr into top of cluster, ch2, ss into ss from prev round, rep from * ending last rep with ss into base of ch2.

Round 3: ss into ch2 and in between next 4sts, * ch5, 4BPtr cl over next 4sts, ch5, ss into sp in between 8th and 9th sts, ch5, work 8BPtr cl into last 4sts of cluster and 1st 4sts on next cluster, ch5, ss into sp between next st, rep from * 3 more times.

Round 4: * ch2, 12tr into top of 1st cluster, ch2, ss into ss from prev round, ch2, 8tr into top of next cluster, ch2, ss into ss from prev round, rep from * to end. Fasten off and weave in ends.

NOW TRY THIS

Two-color block

Work as given for main pattern working Rounds 1–2 in yarn C. Fasten off yarn, then join in yarn B in between 4th and 5th sts. Work Rounds 3–4 as given for main pattern. Fasten off.

Flat petal square

Work as given for main pattern working Rounds 1–2 in yarn B and Rounds 3–4 in yarn E.

Solid square edge

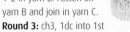

Work as given for main pattern, working Rounds 1–2 in yarn B. Fasten off yarn B and join in yarn C.

Round 3: ch3, 1dc into 1st 2sts, * (3dc, ch3, 3dc) into 1st ch3 sp, work 1dc into each of the next (3dc, ch1 sp, 3dc), ch1sp **, (3dc), rep from * ending last rep at **, ss into top of ch3.

chain reaction

Materials

size G hook

Debbie Bliss Rialto DK in
Baby Pink (A), Light Green (B),
Brown (C), Emerald (D)

Notes

exsc=extended single crochet.

Main pattern: using yarn A, ch17.

Row 1: 1exsc into 3rd ch from hook, 1exsc into each ch to end, turn.

Row 2: ch1, 1sc into front loop of 1st exsc, * ch6, 1sc into front loop of next exsc, rep from * ending with 1sc into front loop of last exsc, turn.

Row 3: ch1, 1exsc into empty loop of 1st exsc, 1exsc into every empty loop of each exsc to end, turn.

Rows 2–3 form pattern; repeat to required length. Fasten off and weave in ends.

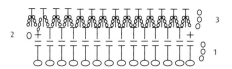

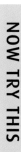

Color variation

Work as given for main pattern using yarn B for Rows 1–2 and yarn C for Rows 3–4, and continue working in stripe sequence as set.

Lightweight chain

Row 1: using yarn D, work as Row 1 of main pattern. **Row 2:** ch1, 1sc into front loop of 1st st, * ch6, 1sc into front loop of next 2sts, rep from * to end.

Aligned chain loops

Work Row 1 as given for main pattern using yarn B. **Row 2:** ch1, 1sc into front loop of 1st exsc, * ch6, 1sc in front loop of next 3 exsc, rep from * to end, turn. **Row 3:** ch1, 1exsc in back loop of 1st st, 1exsc into each back loop to end, turn. Rows 2–3 form the pattern; repeat to required length.

fan stitch

Materials

size G hook

King Cole Smooth Double Knit in
Raspberry (A), Blue (B), Gray (C),
Green (D)

Main pattern: Using yarn A, ch21.

Row1: 5tr into the 6th ch from the hook, * sk2ch, 1dc into next ch, sk2ch, 5tr into next ch, rep from * ending 1dc into last ch, turn.

Row 2: ch3, 2tr into 1st dc, * sk2, 1dc into next tr (center tr of 5), sk2, 5tr into next dc, rep from * ending 3tr into top of tch, turn.

Row 3: ch3, sk3, * 5tr into next dc, sk2, 1dc into next tr (center tr of 5), sk2, rep from * ending 1dc into top of tch, turn.

Rows 2–3 form pattern, repeat to required length. Fasten off and weave in ends.

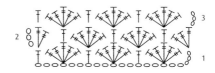

NOW TRY THIS

Half-and-half color
Work as given for main pattern, working Rows 1–5 in yarn A and Rows 6–10 in yarn B.

Four-color stripe
Work as given for main pattern, in a single row stripe using colors A, B, C, and D for 10 rows.

Half double crochet
Using yarn A, ch21. Work as given for main pattern, working each fan using hdc throughout and ch2 for turning chain.

Lace

Use combinations of crochet stitches and
spaces to create light and airy designs
which are typical of many crochet fabrics.

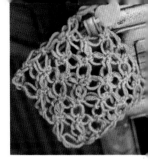

solomon's knot

Materials

size D hook

Debbie Bliss Rialto 4-ply in Emerald (A), Brown (B), Spruce (C)

DMC Starlet (D)

Main pattern: using yarn A, ch2.

Row 1: * draw up loop 1 inch, work 1sc through back strand of elongated loop just made, rep from * 5 more times. This forms the foundation row.

Row 2: work 2 extra elongated loops to turn, work 1sc in center of 4th sc or knot from hook, * (draw loop up 1 inch, work 1sc in back strand of same loop) twice, sk1 knot and work 1sc in 2nd knot, rep from * across row, and end with 1sc in last st. Row 2 forms the pattern; repeat to required length. Fasten off and weave in ends.

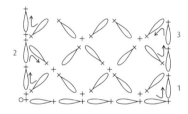

NOW TRY THIS

Little Solomon
Using yarn B, work as given for main pattern but keep loops 1/2 inch long.

Big Solomon
Using yarn C, work as given for main pattern, but keep loops 2 inches long.

Sparkle
Using yarn D, work as given for main pattern.

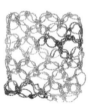

peacock

Materials

size G hook

King Cole Bamboo Cotton DK in Peacock (A), Yellow (B), Damson (C), Moss (D) Aqua (E)

Main pattern: using yarn A, ch21+1.

Row 1: 1sc into 2nd ch from hook, * sk4, 9tr into next ch, sk4, 1sc into next ch, rep from * to end, turn.

Row 2: ch4, 1tr into 1st sc, * ch3, sk4, 1sc into next st (center of 9 tr), ch3, sk4, work (1tr, 1ch, 1tr) into next st, rep from * to end, 2tr into last st, turn.

Row 3: ch1, 1sc in between 2tr, * sk3, 9tr into next st, sk3, 1sc into 1ch in between next 2tr, rep from * to end, 1sc into top of tch, turn.

Rows 2–3 form the pattern; repeat to required length. Fasten off and weave in ends.

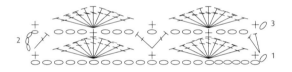

NOW TRY THIS

Large-scale simple peacock stitch

Using yarn A, ch28+1.
Row 1: 1sc in 2nd ch from hook, * sk6, 13exdc (extended double crochet) into next st, sk6, 1sc into next, rep from * to end, turn.
Row 2: ch4, 1exdc into sc, * ch5, 1sc into 7th exdc, ch5 (1exdc, 1ch, 1exdc) into sc, rep from * ending last rep working 2exdc into last st, turn. **Row 3:** ch1, 1sc in between 1st 2exdc, sk5ch, 13exdc into next sc, sk5ch, 1sc into 1ch in between next 2exdc, rep from * ending last rep working 1sc into last st, turn. Rows 2–3 form the pattern; repeat to required length.

Colored peacock feathers

Work as for the main pattern using the following colors: Row 1 in yarn B, Row 2 in yarn A, Row 3 in yarn C, Row 4 in yarn A, Row 5 in yarn D, Row 6 in yarn A, Row 7 in yarn E, and Row 8 in yarn A to complete the pattern.

Framed peacock tails

Using yarn A, ch15+1.
Row 1: work as given for Row 1 of Large-scale simple peacock stitch. Fasten off yarn A and join in yarn E.
Row 2: ch4, 1tr into sc, 1exdc into next st, 1dc into next st, 1hdc into next st, 1sc into each of the next 6sts, 1hdc into next st, 1dc into next, 1exdc into next, 1tr into each of the next 2 sts, turn. **Row 3:** ch3, 1dc into each st to end, turn. Rows 1–3 form the pattern. Repeat to required length.

annette

Materials

size H hook

Rowan Kid Classic in
Lavender Ice (A), Tea Rose (B),
Rosewood (C)

Main pattern: using yarn A, ch19+4 for turning chain.

Row 1: 1dc into 5th ch from hook. * ch1, sk1, 1dc into next ch, rep from * to end, turn.

Row 2: ch4 (counts as 1dc and 1ch), sk1 ch sp, 1dc into top of next st, rep from * (of row 1) working last dc into top of tch, turn.

Row 2 forms pattern; repeat to required length. Fasten off and weave in ends.

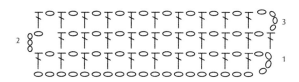

NOW TRY THIS

Offset mesh

Using yarn B, ch21+4 for turning. **Row 1:** work as Row 1 of main pattern. **Row 2:** ch5, sk 1st, 1dc into 1st ch sp, * ch1, sk1, 1dc into next ch1 sp, rep from * to end, working last dc into top of tch, turn. Row 2 forms pattern; repeat Row 2 to required length.

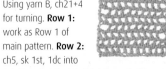

Half double crochet

Using yarn A, ch20+2 for turning. **Row 1:** 1hdc into 3rd ch from hook * ch1, sk1, 1hdc into next ch, rep from * to end, turn.
Row 2: ch2, sk1 st ch sp, 1hdc into top of next st, rep from * working last st into the top of tch, turn. Row 2 forms the pattern; repeat to required length.

Treble crochet

Using yarn C, ch21+5 for turning. **Row 1:** 1tr into 6th ch from hook, * ch1, sk1, 1tr into next ch, rep from * to end, turn. **Row 2:** ch5, sk ch sp, 1tr into top of next st, rep from * working last st into the top of tch, turn. Row 2 forms the pattern; repeat to required length.

seaside

Materials

size G hook: main, Striped color

size D hook: Sparkly

Sublime Baby Cashmere Merino DK in Seasaw (A), Nutkin (B), Puffin (C)

DMC Starlet (D)

Notes

dctog=work a set of double crochet stitches together, over a number of stitches.

Main pattern: Using yarn A, ch27.

Row 1: dc3tog over 4th, 5th 6th ch from hook, * ch1, (1tr into next ch, ch1) twice, (1tr, ch1, 1tr) into next st, (ch1, 1tr into next ch) twice, ch1, dc7tog over next 7sts, rep from * ending with dc4tog over last 4sts, turn.

Row 2: ch3, 1dc into 1st ch sp, * work (1dc into top of tr, 1dc into ch sp) 5 times, 1dc into next tr, work dc2tog over next 2 ch1sps, rep from * ending last rep working dc2tog over last ch sp and top of dc4tog, turn.

Row 3: ch3, sk1, dc3tog over next 3sts, * ch1, (1tr in next st, ch1) twice, (1tr, ch1, 1tr) into next st, (ch1, 1tr into next st) twice, ch1, dc7tog over next 7sts rep from * ending dc4tog over last 4sts, turn.

Rows 2–3 form the pattern; repeat to required length. Fasten off and weave in ends.

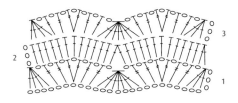

NOW TRY THIS

Striped color

Work as given for main pattern, working Rows 1, 3, 5, and 9 in yarn A and Rows 2, 4, 6, and 8 in yarn B.

Sand, sea, and sky

Using picture as a guide for colors, work as given for main pattern.

Sparkly

Using size D hook, work as given for main pattern using yarn D.

jasper

Materials

size H hook: main

size G hook: Half double crochet, Blocked rows, Fences

Rowan Kid Classic Lavender ice (C)

King Cole Bamboo Cotton DK in Moss (A), Damson (B), Cobalt (D)

buttons for project

Project notes

Coffeepot cozy. Ch multiples of 22 until ch fits around the pot, then add 4 chs. Work as main pattern. Finish with a shell edge and add buttons to fasten.

Main pattern: Using yarn C, ch22+4.

Row 1: 1dc into 6th ch from hook, ch1, sk1, 1dc into next ch, ch1, sk1, * 1dc into each of next 4ch, ch1 **, (sk1, 1dc into next ch, ch1) 3 times, sk1, rep from * to ** once more, sk1, 1dc into last ch, turn.

Row 2: ch4 (counts as 1dc and ch1), sk2, * 1dc into each of next 4sts, ch1, (sk1, 1dc into next st, ch1) 3 times, rep from * ending last rep with 1dc into top of tch, turn.

Row 3: ch3 (counts as 1dc), sk1, * (1dc into next ch1sp, 1dc into next st) twice, 1dc into next ch1sp, ch1, sk1, 1dc into next st, ch1, 1dc into next st, rep from * once more, 1dc into next ch1sp, 1dc into top of tch, turn.

Rows 2–3 form pattern; repeat to required length. Fasten off and weave in ends.

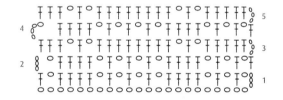

NOW TRY THIS

Half double crochet

Using yarn B, ch20+2. Work as given for main pattern using hdc throughout and ch2 for turning.

Blocked rows

Using yarn A, ch20+4.

Row 1: 1dc into 4th ch from hook, 1dc into each ch to end, turn.

Row 2: ch4, sk2, 1dc into next st, * ch1, sk1, 1dc into next st, rep from * to end, working last dc into turning ch, turn. **Row 3:** ch3, sk1, 1dc into each st to end, turn. Rows 2–3 form the pattern; repeat to required length.

Fences

Using yarn D, ch20+2.

Row 1: 1dc into 4th ch from hook, 1dc into each of next 2ch, * ch2, sk2, 1dc into next ch, rep from * 4 times, 1dc into each of next 2sts.

Row 2: as Row 1 working into sts and ch3sps. Row 2 forms the pattern; repeat to required length.

wagon wheels

Materials

size G hook

Sublime Baby Cashmere Merino Silk DK in Caterpillar (A), Ragdoll (B), Teddy Red (C), Cheeky (D), Pinkaboo (E)

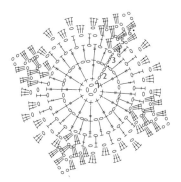

Main pattern: using yarn A, ch4, join with ss to form a ring.

Round 1: ch1 (does not count as st), 12sc into ring, join with ss into ch.

Round 2: ch6 (counts as 1tr and 2ch), 1tr into next st, * ch2, 1tr into next st, rep from * to end, ch2, join with ss into 4th ch at beg of round.

Round 3: ch5 (counts as 1tr and 1ch), * 1tr into ch2sp, ch1, 1tr into next st, ch1, rep from * to end, join with ss into 4th ch at beg of round. Fasten off yarn A and join in yarn B.

Round 4: ch3 (counts as 1dc), 2dc, ch3, 3dc into 1st ch1sp (1st corner worked), ch1, * (1dc, ch1) into each of next 5 ch1sp **, (3dc, ch3, 3dc) into next ch1sp, ch1, rep from * ending last rep at **, join with ss into top of ch.

Round 5: ss into 1st 2sts and 1st ch3sp, ch3 (counts as 1dc), 2dc, ch3, 3dc into same ch3sp (1st corner worked), * ch1, 3dc into next ch1sp, sk next ch1sp, ch1, (3dc into next ch1sp, ch1) twice, sk next ch sp, 3dc into next ch1sp, ch1 **, work (3dc, ch3, 3dc) into next ch3sp, rep from * ending last rep at **, join with ss into top of ch3. Ss into next 2sts and ch3sp. Fasten off yarn B and join in yarn C.

Round 6: ch3 (counts as 1dc), 2dc into 1st ch3sp, ch3, 3dc into same sp, (1st corner worked), * 3dc into each of the next 4 ch1sps **, (3dc, ch3, 3dc) into next ch3sp, rep from * ending last rep at **, join with ss into top of ch3. Fasten off and weave in ends.

NOW TRY THIS

Solid edge

Work Rounds 1–3 as given for main pattern using yarn C. Change to yarn B. **Rounds 4–5:** ss into ch sp, ch3, 2dc into same sp *dc into top of next st, dc into ch sp 5 times, 3dc, ch3, 3dc into next ch sp*, repeat from * to end, ss into top of ch3.

Filet edge

Work Rounds 1–4 as given for main pattern.
Round 5: ch4 (counts as 1dc and ch1), * sk1, 1dc into next st, ch1, sk1, 2dc, ch3, 2dc into next ch3sp (1st corner worked), ch1, sk1, 1dc into next st, ch1, (1dc, ch1) into next 6 ch1sp, rep from * ending last rep with (1dc, ch1) into 5 ch1sp, join with ss into 3rd of ch4 at beg of round.

Cluster center

With yarn D, ch4, join with ss to form a ring.
Round 1: ch2 (counts as 1dc), 2dc cl into ring, * ch2, 3dc cl into ring, rep from * 4 more times, ch2, join with ss into top of 1st cluster. Change to yarn C. **Round 2:** ch5 (counts as 1tr and ch2), 1tr into ch2sp, * ch2, 1tr in top of next cl, ch2, 1tr into next ch2sp, rep from * 4 more times, ch2, ss into 3rd of ch4 at beg of the round. Change to Round E.
Rounds 3–4: work as given for filet edge.

54

maude

Materials

size G hook

King Cole Bamboo Cotton DK in Oyster (A), Rose (B), Aqua (C), Damson (D), Opal (E)

Main pattern: using yarn A, ch6, join with ss to form a ring.

Round 1: ch1 (does not count as st), 12sc into ring, join with ss into ch1.

Round 2: ch4 (counts as 1dc and ch1), * 1dc into next st, ch1, rep from * to end, join with ss into 3rd ch of ch4.

Round 3: ch3 (counts as 1dc), 2dc into 1st ch sp, ch1, * 3dc into next ch sp, ch1, rep from * to end, join with ss into 3rd of ch4. Ss into each of next 2dc and ch sp.

Round 4: ch5 (counts as 1dc and ch2), sk next st, 1dc into ch1sp, * ch2, sk next st, 1dc into next st, ch2, sk next st, 1dc into ch sp, rep from * ending last rep with ch2, ss into 3rd ch of 5ch at beg of round.

Round 5: ch1, 3sc into ch2sp,* 3sc into next ch2sp, rep from * to end, join with ss into ch1.

Round 6: ch3 (counts as 1dc), 2dc, ch3, 3dc into 1st st, * ch1, sk2, 3hdc into next st, ch1, (sk2, 3hdc into next st, ch1) 3 times, sk2, 3hdc into next st, sk2, 3dc, ch3, 3dc into next st, rep from * to end, join with ss into top of ch3. Fasten off and weave in ends.

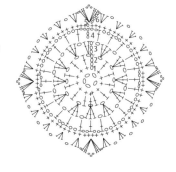

NOW TRY THIS

Two-color

Work as given for main pattern.
Rounds 1–3: using yarn A. **Rounds 4–6:** using yarn B.

Multicolor

Work as given for main pattern.
Round 1: using yarn A. **Round 2:** using yarn B. **Round 3:** using yarn C. **Round 4:** using yarn D. **Rounds 5–6:** using yarn E.

Alternating colors

Work as given for main pattern. **Rounds 1, 3, and 5:** using yarn A. **Rounds 2 and 4:** using yarn C. **Round 6:** using yarn C, ch2, work 1hdc into next 3sts, 1sc into each of next 9sts, 1hdc into next 4sts, * (3dc, ch2, 3dc) into next st, 1hdc into each of next 4sts, 1sc into each of next 9sts, 1hdc into each of next 4sts, rep from * 3 more times, join with a ss into top of ch2. Fasten off.

Materials

size G hook

Patons DK cotton in
White (A), Raffia (B), Orchard (C),
Lilac (D), Foxglove (E), Denim (F),
Nougat (G), Jade (H)

dot

Main pattern: Using yarn A, ch20.

Row 1: 1sc into 2nd ch from hook, * ch2, sk2, 1sc into next ch, rep from * to end, joining yarn B on last st, turn; do not break yarn A.

Row 2: using yarn B, ch4, * 3dc into ch2sp, ch1, rep from * to end, turn, do not break yarn B.

Row 3: return to beginning of Row 2, draw yarn A through under 4th of 4ch, ch1 (counts as 1sc) * ch2, 1sc into ch1sp, rep from * to end, drawing yarn B through last st, turn.

Row 4: using yarn B, work as Row 2.

Rep Rows 3–4 throughout, always starting each row at the end where the correct color was left.

Rows 3–4 form pattern; repeat these rows, working each row in correct color.

Fasten off and weave in ends.

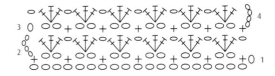

NOW TRY THIS

Different colored dots

Work Rows 1 and 3 in alternating colors e.g. yarns B–H and Rows 2 and 4 in yarn A.

Treble crochet

Using yarns A and H, work as given for main pattern, using tr throughout and ch4 for turning.

More chains between dots

Using yarn A for odd rows and yarn C for even rows work as follows: on Rows 1 and 3, work from * ch4, sk4 to spread dots out along the rows.

58

starry eyed

Materials

size G hook

Sublime Extra Fine Merino Wool DK in Splash (A), Vanilla (B), Salty Gray (C), Piglet (D)

Main pattern: using yarn A, ch24.

Row 1: 1dc into 8th ch from hook to create corner loop, (ch1, 1dc) 3 times into same ch (1 shell has been worked), * sk 3ch, 1dc into next ch, (ch1, 1dc) 3 times into same st, rep from * to last ch4, sk3, 1dc into last ch, turn.

Row 2: ch3, * 1dc into middle of next shell, (ch1, 1dc) 3 times into same ch sp, rep from * to last st, 1dc into middle of corner loop space, turn.

Row 2 forms the pattern. Repeat to required length. Fasten off and weave in ends.

NOW TRY THIS

Color variation

Work as given for main pattern, working Row 1 in yarn A, Row 2 in yarn B, Row 3 in yarn C. Repeat stripe pattern to required length.

Half double crochet

Using yarn B, ch25.
Row 1: 1hdc into 9th st from hook, work as given for main pattern, working in hdc throughout with ch2 for turning.

Treble crochet

Using yarn C, ch26. **Row 1:** 1tr into 10th ch from hook, work as given for main pattern, working in tr throughout with ch4 for turning.

rainbow

Materials

size G hook

Sublime Baby Cashmere Merino Silk DK in
Ragdoll (A), Cheeky (B), Puffin (C)
Caterpillar (D), Puzzle (E), Teddy Red (F),
Vanilla (G)

Main pattern: with yarn A, make a magic circle (see page 11).

Round 1: * 1ch, (1sc, 1hdc, 2dc) into ring, remove hook but do not cut yarn, leaving a long loop, join in yarn B, repeat from *, rep with yarn C and D. Pull tail to close magic circle.

Round 2: with yarn A, * 2dc into 1st st, 1dc into next st, 2dc into next st, 1dc into next st, rep from * with B, C, and D.

Round 3: with yarn A, * ch2, 1dc into next dc, sk1, 2dc into each of next 2 sts, sk1, 1dc, rep from * with B, C, and D.

Round 4: with yarn A, * 2dc, ch2, 2dc into ch sp, sk1, ch1, work (2dc in next st) 3 times, rep from * with B, C, and D.

Round 5: with yarn A, * ch1, (3dc, ch2, 3dc) into ch2sp, sk2, ch1, 2dc in ch1 sp, sk2, ch1, 1hdc, 1sc into ch sp, sk2, ch1, (1sc, ss) into last ch1sp, rep from * with B, C, and D. Fasten off and weave in ends.

NOW TRY THIS

Solid spiral granny square

Work Rounds 1–2 as given for main pattern. **Round 3:** with yarn B, * ch2, 2dc into 1st st, 1dc into each of next 5sts, rep from * with E, F, and G. **Round 4:** with yarn B, * ch1, 2dc, ch2, 2dc in ch sp, 1dc into each of next 7sts, rep from * with E, F, and G. **Round 5:** with yarn B, * work 1dc into next st, 1hdc into next st, 1sc into next st, ss into next st, fasten off, rep from * with colors E, F, and G.

Two-color spiral

Using yarn E, ch6, join with ss to form a ring. **Round 1:** with yarn E, * ch3, 5dc into ring, rep from * with yarn B. **Round 2:** with yarn E, * 2dc into top of ch3, 2dc into each of next 4sts, rep from * with yarn B. **Round 3:** with E, * work (1dc into next st, 2dc into next st) 5 times, rep from * with yarn B. **Round 4:** with E, * work (1dc into next st, 2dc into next st) 3 times, 2dc into next st, 1dc into next st, 1hdc in each of next 3sts, 1sc into each of next 2sts, ss into next st, rep from * with yarn B.

Spiral hexagon

Using yarn D, ch6, join with ss to form a ring. **Round 1:** 12sc into ring, place marker. [12 sts] **Round 2:** * 2sc into each st around, place marker. [24 sts] **Round 3:** (1sc into each of next 3sts, ch3, sk1) 6 times. **Round 4:** (1sc into each of next 4sts, 2sc into ch3sp, ch3) 6 times. **Round 5:** (1sc into each of next 5sts, 2sc into ch3sp, ch3) 6 times.

vintage stripes

Materials

size G hook

Sublime Baby Cashmere Merino Silk DK in
Gooseberry (A), Puffin (B), Piglet (C)

Main pattern: using yarn A, ch28+3.
Row 1: 1dc into 4th ch from hook, sk2, * 3dc into next ch, sk2, rep from * ending,
2dc into last ch, turn.
Row 2: ch3, sk2, 3dc into 1st sp, * sk3, 3dc into next sp, rep from * to end, work
1dc into top of ch3, turn.
Row 3: ch3, 1dc into 1st sp, * sk3, 3dc into next sp, rep from * 6 more times, sk3,
2dc into top of ch3, turn.
Rows 2–3 form the pattern; repeat to required length. Fasten off and weave in ends.

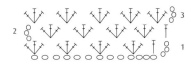

**Two-color
stripes**
Work as given for main
pattern, working odd
rows in yarn B and
even rows in yarn A.
Fasten off.

Cluster stripe
Using yarn C, ch28+3
ch for turning. **Row
1:** 2dc cl into 4th ch
from hook, ch2, sk2, *
3dc cl into next ch, ch2, sk2, rep from * to
end, turn. **Row 2:** ch3, 3dc cl into 1st ch2
sp, ch2, * 3dc cl into next ch2sp, rep from
* ending last rep with 3dc cl into top of
ch3, turn. Repeat Row 2 to required length.
Fasten off.

Puff stitch
Using yarn B, work
pattern as given
for Cluster stripe,
working puff stitches
(see page 12)
throughout.

wedges

Materials

size G hook

King Cole Bamboo Cotton DK in Opal (A), Cobalt (B), Cream (C)

Notes

1fpttr – front post triple treble

1fp quad tr – front post quadruple treble

1fp quin tr – front post quintuple treble

Main pattern: using yarn A, ch16.

Row 1: 1dc into 4th ch from hook, 1dc into each ch to end, turn.

Row 2: ch3, 1dc into each st to end, turn.

Row 3: ch3, * sk3, work (1fpttr, 1fp quad tr, 1fp quin tr) around stem of next st on row below, 1tr.

Rows 2–3 form the pattern; repeat to required length, ending on Row 2. Fasten off and weave in ends.

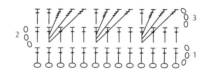

Color variation

Work as given for main pattern, with Rows 1–2 in yarn B and Row 3 in yarn A.

Big to small

Using yarn C, ch16.

Rows 1–2: work as for main pattern.

Row 3: ch3, * sk3, work (3fptr) around same st on prev row, 1dc in same st, rep from * to last st, 1dc into last st, turn. Rows 2–3 form the pattern. Repeat to required length, ending on Row 2.

Wings

Using yarn C, ch20.

Rows 1–2: work as given for main pattern. Fasten off yarn C and join in yarn B. **Row 3:** ch3, * sk3, work 3fptr around same st on prev row, 1dc in same st, 1dc in next st, 3fptr around next st on prev row, rep from * to last st, 1dc, turn. Fasten off yarn B and join in yarn C. **Row 4:** as Row 2. **Row 5:** as Row 3. **Row 6:** as Row 2.

Shapes

Crochet stitches can be used to create many shapes by increasing or decreasing as you work in the round or as rows. Shapes can also be made within a square or circle.

twinkle

Materials

size G hook

Sublime Extra Fine Merino Wool DK in Roasted Pepper (A), Pistachio (B)

A DK-weight color-changing yarn such as Colinette Cadenza in Sweet Dreams (C)

Main pattern: using yarn A, ch4, join with ss to form a ring.

Round 1: ch3 (counts as 1dc), 9dc into ring, join with ss into ch3.

Round 2: * ch5, 1sc into 2nd ch from hook, work into rem 3ch as follows, 1hdc into next ch, 1dc into next ch, 1tr into last ch, sk1, ss into next st, rep from * to end, join with ss into base of ch5. Fasten off and weave in ends.

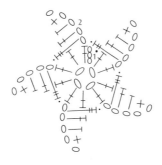

NOW TRY THIS

Red-centered star

Work as given for main pattern, Round 1 in yarn A and round 2 in yarn B.

Mix it up

Using 2 separate ends of yarn B held together as one, work as given for main pattern. Add a Lurex yarn for a touch of sparkle or work each point in a different color.

Starfish

Using yarn C, work Round 1 as given for main pattern. **Round 2:** * ch10, 1sc into 3rd ch from hook, work as follows into rem 9ch, 1sc into next ch, 1hdc into each of next 2ch, 1dc into each of next 2ch, 1tr into each of last 2ch, sk1, ss into next st, rep from * to end, join with ss into base of beg ch10.

doilies

Materials

size G hook

King Cole Bamboo Cotton DK in Yellow (A), Moss (B), Oyster (C), Plum (D)

Notes:

MP=make picot.

Main pattern: using yarn A, ch5, join with ss to form a ring.

Round 1: ch6 (counts as 1tr and ch2), 1tr into ring, * ch2, 1tr into ring, rep from * 6 more times, join with ss to 4th ch of ch6.

Round 2: ss into first ch2sp, ch4, 4tr into same ch2sp, ch2, * 5tr into next ch2sp, ch2, rep from * to end, join with ss into top of tch.

Round 3: ch4, 1tr into each of next 4 sts, * (1tr, ch3, 1tr) into ch2sp **, 1tr into each of next 5sts, rep from * ending last rep at **, join with ss to top of tch, turn.

Round 4: ch1, ss into 1st st, * 1sc into next ch3sp, 6ch, sk1, tr5tog over next 5sts, ch6, 1sc into next ch3sp, rep from * to end, join with ss into sc at beg of row, turn.

Round 5: ch4, ss into 3rd ch from hook, MP, * 8sc into ch6sp, 1sc into top of tr5tog, (MP) 3 times, 1sc into top of tr5tog, 8sc into next ch6sp, 1sc into next st, MP, rep from * to end, join with ss into base of 1st picot. Fasten off and weave in ends.

NOW TRY THIS

Mini star doily

Using yarn C, ch4, join with ss to form a ring. **Round 1:** ch3 (counts as 1dc), 11dc into ring, join with ss into top of tch. **Round 2:** ch5 (counts as 1dc and ch2), 1dc into next chsp, ch2, 1dc into next st, ch2 rep from * to end, join with ss into top of tch. **Round 3:** ss into first ch2sp, work (1sc, 1hdc, 3ch, 1hdc, 1sc) into next and every following ch2sp to end, join with ss into top of sc at beg of round. **Round 4:** ss into each of next 2sts and into ch3sp, * ch5, 1sc into ch3sp, rep from * to end, join with ss into base of ch5. **Round 5:** work 3sc, MP, 2sc into each ch sp around.

Simple dinky doily

Using yarn D, ch8, join with ss to form a ring. **Round 1:** ch3 (counts as 1dc), 2dc cl into ring, ch2, * 3dc cl into ring, ch2, rep from * 6 more times, join with ss into ch3. **Round 2:** ch4 (counts as 1dc, ch1), 1dc into 1st chsp, ch2, (1dc, 1ch, 1dc) into each chsp around. Join with ss into 3rd of ch4. **Round 3:** ch3 (counts as 1dc), 1dc, ch3, 2dc into ch2sp, 1sc into next ch2sp, * (2dc, ch3, 2dc) into next ch2sp, 1sc into next ch2sp, rep from * to end, join with ss into ch3.

Mini doily

Using yarn B, ch4, join with ss to form a ring. **Round 1:** work as given for main pattern in dc, with ch5 at beg of round. **Round 2:** work as given for main pattern, with ch3 at beg of round, turn at the end of this round. **Round 3:** ch1, sc into 1st chsp, ch4, sk2, * ch4, sk2, tr3tog, ch4, 1sc into next ch2sp, rep from * to end, join with ss into sc at beg of round, turn. **Round 4:** MP * 4sc into ch4sp, 1sc into top of tr3tog, MP, 1sc into top of tr3tog, 4sc into ch4sp, 1sc into next st, MP, rep from * to end, join with ss into base of 1st picot.

evening sunset

Materials

size G hook

King Cole Bamboo Cotton DK in Yellow (A), Aqua (B), Red (C), White (D), Plum (E)

pillow pad for project

Project notes

Pillow. Make 12 squares using 4 colors. Make 2 squares of each color combination and join at stage 4 of the pattern, using the "on-the-go" method (see page 15). For the back piece of the cover, make a chain the length of the pillow front and work in granny stripes. With wrong sides together, join 2 sides using single crochet, inserting pillow pad before crocheting up the last side.

Main pattern: using yarn B, ch5, join with ss to form a ring.

Round 1: ch3 (counts as 1dc), 11dc into ring, join with ss into ch3. Fasten off.

Round 2: join in yarn C in between 1st and 2nd sts, ch3 (counts as 1dc), 1dc into same sp, work 2dc in between next and every st following to end, working last 2sts in between last st and ch3, join with ss into ch3. Fasten off.

Round 3: join in yarn A in between 1st and 2nd sts, ch3 (counts as 1dc), 2dc into same sp, work 3dc in between next and every st to end, working last 3sts in between last st and ch3, join with ss into ch3. Fasten off.

Round 4: join in yarn D into next 2sts and in between next 2sts, ch3 (counts as 1dc), 2dc, ch3, 3dc into same sp (1st corner worked), * (sk3, 3dc in between next 2sts) twice **, sk3, work (3dc, ch3, 3dc) in between next 2sts, rep from * ending last rep at **, join with ss into ch3. Fasten off and weave in ends.

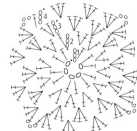

NOW TRY THIS

Cluster stitch

Using yarn B, ch5, join with ss to form a ring.

Round 1: work as given for main pattern.

Round 2: ss into 1st chsp, ch2, * 2dc cl into ch1sp, ch3 * 3dc in between next 2sts, ch1, rep from * to end working last cluster in between last st and ch2, join with ss into ch2.

Round 3: ss into first chsp, ch2, *2dc cluster into ch1sp, ch3 * 3dc in between next 2sts, ch3, rep from * to end working last cluster in between last st and ch2, join with ss into ch2. Fasten off yarn B and join in yarn E.

Round 4: work as for the main pattern.

Combination textured sunburst

Using yarn C, ch5, join with ss to form a ring.

Round 1: as for the main pattern. **Round 2:** ss in between 1st and 2nd sts, ch2, 1 puff stitch (see page 12) into same sp, ch1, * 1 puff stitch in between next 2sts, ch1, rep from * to end working last cluster in between last st and ch2, join with ss into ch2. **Round 3:** ss into 1st chsp, ch2, 2dc cl into same sp, ch3, * 3dc into next 2sts, ch3 *, rep to end working last cluster into last ch2sp. Fasten off yarn C and join in yarn E. **Round 4:** work as for the main pattern.

Reverse colors

Work as given for main pattern, using the colors in reverse order.

Materials

size G hook

Debbie Bliss Cotton DK in
Green (A), Red (B), Blue (C),
Pigeon (D)

flora

Main pattern: using yarn A, ch3, join with ss to form a ring.
Round 1: ch1 (does not count as 1sc), 10sc into the ring, join with ss in ch1.
Round 2: * ch2, work (1hdc, 1dc, 1tr, 1dc, 1hdc) into next st, ch2, 1sc into next st, rep from * 4 more times. Fasten off yarn and weave in ends.

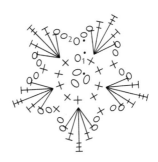

NOW TRY THIS

Two-color flower

Work as given for main pattern, working Round 1 in yarn A and Round 2 in yarn B.

Open flower

Using yarn C, ch3, join with ss to form ring. **Round 1:** ch5 (counts as 1dc and 2ch), * 1dc, ch2, rep from * to end, join with ss to 3rd of ch5. **Round 2:** work as Round 2 of main pattern.

Pretty violet

Using yarn D, ch 4, join with ss to form ring. **Round 1:** work as Round 1 of main pattern. **Round 2:** * ch4, sk1, 1sc into next st, rep from * ending last rep with ss into base of ch4. **Round 3:** ch1 (counts as 1ch), 4dc into 1st ch4 loop, * ss into next st, 5dc into next ch4 loop, rep from * to end, ss into ch1.

70

diamonds are forever

Materials

size G hook

Debbie Bliss Rialto DK in
Duck Egg (A), Gold (B), Emerald (C),
Scarlet (D)

Main pattern: using yarn D, ch2.

Row 1: 2sc into 2nd ch from hook, turn.

Row 2: ch1 (does not count as stitch), 1sc into first st, 2sc into 2nd st, turn.

Row 3: ch1 (does not count as stitch), 1sc into 1st st, 1sc into 2nd st, 2sc into last st, turn.

Rows 4-10 (inc): ch1 (does not count as stitch), 2sc into 1st st, work 1sc into each st to the last st, 2sc into last st, turn.

Rows 11–22 (dec): ch1, sk1, 1sc into next st, 1sc into each st to end turn. Fasten off and weave in ends.

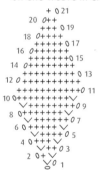

Half double crochet diamond

Using yarn A, ch3.

Row 1: 2hdc into 3rd ch from hook, turn. Work as given for main pattern, working hdc throughout and ch2 for turning.

Double crochet

Using yarn B, ch4. **Row 1:** 2dc into 4th ch from hook, turn. **Rows 2–10:** increasing as given for main pattern, working dc throughout and ch3 for turning chain. **Rows 11–20 (dec):** ch3 (counts as 1dc), sk1, dc2tog, 1dc into each st to last 3sts, dc2tog, 1dc into last st, turn.

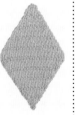

Spike stitch diamond

Using yarn C, work as given for main pattern keeping inc and dec correct. Work every 4th row as spike stitch (sp st) in yarn A. **Spike rows:** work 2sts as in main pattern, * 1sp st (work sc into same st 1 row below), 1sc into next st, rep from * to last 2sts, 1sc into each of last 2sts, turn.

polka

Materials

size G hook

Sublime Baby Cashmere Merino Silk
DK in Seesaw (A), Little Miss Plum (B),
Caterpillar (C), Ragdoll (D), Piglet (E),
Puffin (F)

Main pattern: using yarn B, ch5, join with ss to form a ring.

Round 1: ch2 (counts as 1hdc), 11hdc into ring, join with ss into ch2.

Round 2: ch2 (counts as 1hdc), 1hdc in 1st st, 2hdc in each st to end, join with ss into ch2.

Round 3: ch2 (counts as 1hdc), 1hdc into 1st st, * 1hdc into next st, 2hdc into next, rep from * to last st, 1hdc into last st, join with ss into ch2. Fasten off yarn B and join in yarn A.

Round 4: ch4 (counts as 1dc and ch1), 1dc into same st (1st corner worked), * 1hdc into each of next 8 sts, work (1dc, ch2, 1dc) into next st, rep from * twice more, 1hdc into each of last 8 sts, join with ss into 2nd ch of ch3.

Rounds 5 and 6: ss into 1st corner, ch3 (counts as 1dc), work (1dc, 3ch, 2dc) into same sp, * work 1hdc into each st to next corner, work (2dc, 3ch, 2dc) into next corner sp, rep from * twice more, then work 1hdc into each st to end, join with ss into ch2. Fasten off and weave in ends.

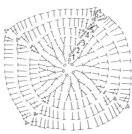

NOW TRY THIS

Puffed center

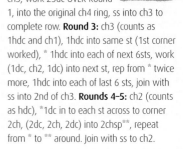

Using yarn C, begin and work **Round 1:** work as for main pattern. **Round 2:** ch3, work 23dc OVER Round 1, into the original ch4 ring, ss into ch3 to complete row. **Round 3:** ch3 (counts as 1hdc and ch1), 1hdc into same st (1st corner worked), * 1hdc into each of next 6sts, work (1dc, ch2, 1dc) into next st, rep from * twice more, 1hdc into each of last 6 sts, join with ss into 2nd of ch3. **Rounds 4–5:** ch2 (counts as hdc), *1dc in to each st across to corner 2ch, (2dc, 2ch, 2dc) into 2chsp**, repeat from * to ** around. Join with ss to ch2.

Rounded square

Using yarn E, work as given for main pattern for Rounds 1–4. Fasten off yarn E and join in yarn F. **Round 5:** ss into 1st corner, ch3 (counts as 1dc), work (1tr, 1dc) into same sp, * work 1hdc into each st to next corner, work (1dc, 1tr, 1dc) into next corner sp, rep from * twice more, then work 1hdc into each st to end, join with ss into ch2. **Round 6:** *ch2, (1dc, 1tr, 1dc) into corner chsp, 1hdc into each st across to chsp,** rep from * to ** 3 times more.

Granny polka dot

Using yarn D, work as given for main pattern for Rounds 1–3.

Round 4: join in yarn C. ch3 (counts as 1dc), (1dc, ch3, 2dc) into same st, (ch1, sk2, 3dc into next st) twice, *(2dc, ch3, 2dc) into next st, ch1, sk2, (3dc into next st, ch1, sk2) twice ** rep from * to ** twice more, join with ss to ch3.

Round 5: ss into chsp, ch3 (counts as 1dc), (2dc, ch3, 3dc) into chsp, (ch1, 3dc into next chsp) three times, *(3dc, ch3, 3dc) into next chsp, (3dc, ch1) into each of next 3chsp**, rep from * to ** twice, join with ss to ch3.

in bloom

Materials

size G hook: main, Two-color flower with 13 petals, and Lacy flower coaster

size H hook: Sunflower

King Cole Bamboo Cotton DK in White (A), Red (B), Moss (C), Opal (D), Debbie Bliss Cotton DK in Brown (E) Rowan Cotton Glace in Persimmon (F)

Project notes

Coasters. Make up 6 of the main pattern for a set.

Main pattern: using yarn A, ch3 and join with ss to form a ring.

Round 1: ch3 (counts as 1dc), 9dc into ring, join with ss into ch3.

Round 2: ch3 (counts as 1dc), 1dc into same st, 2dc into each st to end, join with ss, into ch3.

Round 3: ch3 (counts as 1dc), 2dc into next st, * 1dc into next st, 2dc into next st **, rep from * to ** 8 times more, join with ss into ch3.

Round 4: work as given for Round 2.

Round 5: * sk2, 5dc into next st, sk2, ss to next st (1st petal worked), rep from * to end, working last rep with ss into 1st ch of 5dc at beg of round. Fasten off and weave in ends.

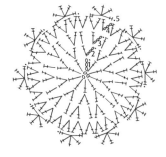

Two-color flower with 13 petals

Using yarn B, ch3, join with ss to form a ring. **Round 1:** ch3 (counts as 1dc), 12dc into ring, join with ss to ch3. [13 sts] **Round 2:** ch3 (counts as 1dc), 1dc into first st, 2dc into each rem st around, join with ss to ch3. [26sts] **Round 3:** ch3 (counts as 1dc), 2dc into next st, *1dc into next st, 2dc into next st**, rep from * to ** 11 times more, join with ss to ch3. [39 sts] **Round 4:** ch1 (counts as 1st sc), 1sc into each st to end, join with ss into ch1. **Round 5:** * ch1, work (1hdc, 1dc) into next st and (1dc, 1hdc) into next st, ch1, ss into next st, rep from * ending last rep with ss into base of ch1.

Lacy flower coaster

Using yarn D, ch4, join with ss to form a ring. **Round 1:** ch3, 11dc into ring, join with ss. **Round 2:** ch3, 1dc into same st, 2dc into each rem st around, join with ss. **Round 3:** ch5 (count as 1dc, 2ch), (1dc, 2ch) into each st around, join with ss. **Round 4:** ch3 (counts as 1dc), (3dc into chsp, 1dc into dc) around, 3dc into last ch sp, join with ss. **Round 5:** ch1, *1dc into first st, sk2, 7dc into next st, sk2** repeat from * to ** 7 times more.

Sunflower

Using yarn E, ch3, join with ss to form a ring. **Rounds 1–3:** work as given for two-color flower with 13 petals. Fasten off yarn E and join in yarn F. **Round 4:** ch3 (counts as 1dc), 1dc into same st, ch2, sk2, * 2dc into next st, ch2, sk1 ** rep from * to ** 8 times, join with ss into ch3. **Round 5:** 3dc, 3ch, 3dc into 1st ch sp, * ss into next ch sp work (3dc, ch3, 3dc) into next ch sp, rep from * ending last rep with ss into top of 1st of st at beg of round.

posy

Materials

size H hook

Rowan All Seasons Cotton in
Blush (A), Plum (B), Hedge (C)

brooch pin and button for project

Project notes

Flower brooch. Attach a brooch pin for an
attractive brooch or corsage for a bag or
pillow. Sew a button to the center-front of
the posy.

Main pattern: using yarn A, ch4 and join with ss to form a ring.

Round 1: ch3 (counts as 1dc), 11dc into ring, join with ss into ch3.

Round 2: ch1, 3dc into next st (1st petal worked), ch1, ss into next st, rep from *
to end, ss into ch1.

Work next round at the back of work to create
6 loops.

Round 3: ch3, sk petal, 1sc into back of ss, rep
from * to end, join with ss into ch3.

Round 4: ch1, 5dc into 1st ch3 loop, ch1, 1sc
into next st, * ch1, 5dc into next ch3 loop, 1sc
into next st, ch1, rep from * to end, join with ss
into ch1. Fasten off and weave in ends.

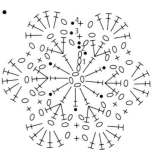

Two-tone flower

Work as given for main
pattern working Rounds
1–3 in yarn A and
Round 4 in yarn B.

Starry flower

Using yarn C, ch4, join
with ss. **Round 1:** ch2
(counts as 1hdc), 11hdc
into ring, join with ss
into ch2. **Round 2:** *
ch1, work (1hdc, 1dc, 1hdc) into next st,
ch1, ss into next st, rep from * to end, ss
into ch1. Work next round at the back of
work to create 6 loops. **Round 3:** ch3, sk
petal, 1sc into back of ss, rep from * to end,
join with ss into ch3. **Round 4:** * ch1, work
(1hdc, 1dc, 1tr, 1dc, 1hdc) into ch3 loop,
ch1, 1sc into next st, rep from * to end, join
with ss into ch1.

Pansy

Using yarn B, ch4, join
with ss to form a ring.

Round 1: * ch4, 3tr
into ring, ch4, ss to ring
(1st petal worked), rep
from * 3 more times making 4 petals in
total. Work next round at the back of work
to create 4 loops. **Round 2:** ch1, ss into back
of next st, ch1, 1sc into next st, * ch2, work
1sc into back of the middle st of next petal,
rep from * ending last rep with ss into ch1.

Round 3: * work (ch4, 4tr, ch4) into ch2loop,
ss into next st, rep from * ending last rep
with ss into base of ch4.

rectangles

Materials

size G hook

Debbie Bliss Cotton DK in Red (A), Green (B), Gray (C), Pale Blue (D)

Project notes

"Paper" chain: Make up 12 rectangles then sew up the ends with mattress stitch, interlocking the rectangles as you go. Increase the number of rectangles for a longer chain.

Main pattern: ch30+1 for turning.

Row 1: sk1,1sc into each ch to end, working last sc into top of turning ch, turn.

Row 2: ch1, sk1, 1sc into each sc to end, working last sc into top of turning ch, turn.

Rows 3–4: repeat Row 2. Fasten off and weave in ends.

NOW TRY THIS

Two-color rectangles

Using yarn B, work as given for main pattern. Then work a row of contrasting sc all around the edge; join in yarn A, ch1, then work 1sc into every st, 3sc into the corner sts. Join with ss.

Ribbed rectangles

Using yarn C, ch30+3 for turning. **Row 1:** 1dc into 4th ch from hook, 1dc into each ch to end, turn. **Row 2:** ch3, 1dc into back loop of 1st st, 1dc into back loop of each st to end, turn. Repeat Row 2 twice more.

Granny rectangles

Using yarn A, ch 20+3 for turning. **Round 1:** ch3, 1dc into first ch, * sk2, 3dc into next ch, rep from * 5 times, sk2, work (2dc, ch3, 3dc, ch3, 2dc) into last ch (corner worked), work back along the underside of ch to match top as foll: ** sk2, 3dc into next ch, rep from ** 5 times, work (2dc, ch3, 3dc) into 1st ch, ss into ch3. Fasten off yarn A and join in yarn D ch3sp. **Round 2:** ch3, 2dc, ch3, 3dc into corner, work 3dc into each ch sp and 3dc, ch3, 3dc into ch3sp around the outer edge.

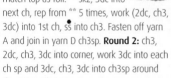

bunting

Materials

size G hook

Debbie Bliss Cotton DK in
Plum (A), Teal (B), Hot Pink (C),
Apple Green (D), Mushroom (E)

Project notes

Bunting. Make up 2 triangles in each color for
bunting. Make a chain of 20, then sc along the
top of the triangles, with 10ch between each
triangle.

Main pattern: using yarn A, ch15+2 for turning.

Row 1: 1hdc into 3rd ch from hook, 1hdc into each ch to end, turn.

Row 2: ch2, sk1, 1hdc into each st to last 2sts, hdc2tog, turn.

Row 3: ch2, 1hdc into each st to end, turn.

Rows 2–3 form decrease pattern; repeat these rows until 5sts remain.

Next row: ch2, hdc2tog, 1hdc, hdc2tog, turn.

Next row: ch2, hdc3tog. Fasten off and weave in ends.

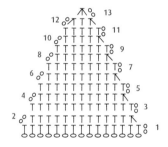

Picot border

Using yarn A, work triangle as for main pattern. Join in yarn E to right hand top corner of triangle, work picot edge as follows: ch1, 1sc into 1st st, * sk1, ch3, 1sc into next st, rep from * around the triangle. Join to 1st st with a ss.

Spike stitch stripes

Using yarn B, ch16. **Row 1:** 1sc in 2nd ch from hook, 1sc into each st across, turn. **Rows 2 & 4:** ch1, sk1, 1sc in each st across to last 2sts, sc2tog, turn. **Row 3:** 1sc into each st across, turn. **Row 5 Spike stitch row:** change to yarn C. ch1, *1dc into next st, spike stitch (SP) into next st (1dc into row below)** repeat from * to ** across, turn. Rows 2–5 set the pattern. Cont in patt until 2sts remain, sc2tog.

Stripes

Work triangle as main pattern using sc throughout and ch1 for turning. Work dec on every 2nd row with sc2tog at beg and end of row. Keeping pattern correct work a 2-row stripe throughout starting with yarn C, then yarn D.

stella

Materials

size G hook

Sublime Baby Cashmere Merino Silk DK
in Seesaw (A), Vanilla (B), Teddy Red (C)

Main pattern: using yarn A, ch4, join with ss to form a ring.
Round 1: ch3 (counts as 1st dc), 2dc into ring, * ch3, 3dc into ring, rep from * once more, ch3, join with ss into top of ch3.
Round 2: ss along and into first ch3sp. Ch3 (counts as 1st dc) work (2dc, ch4, 3dc) into first ch sp,* ch3, (3dc, ch4, 3dc) into next ch3sp, rep from * once more, 3ch, join with ss into top of ch3.
Round 3: ss along and into 1st ch3sp, ch3 (counts as 1st dc), work (2dc, ch4, 3dc) into same sp, * 3ch, 3dc into next ch3sp, 3ch, (3dc, ch4, 3dc) into next ch3sp, rep from * once more, 3ch, join with ss into top of ch3. Fasten off and weave in ends.

NOW TRY THIS

Tri-color triangle
Using yarn A, ch4, join with ss to form a ring. Work as given for main pattern with Round 1 in yarn A, Round 2 in yarn B, and Round 3 in yarn C.

Solid DC triangle
Using yarn C, ch4, join with ss to form a ring.
Row 1: work as given for main pattern. **Row 2:** ch3 (counts as 1dc), 1dc into each of next 2sts, * 2dc, ch3, 2dc into 1st ch3sp, 1dc into each of next 3sts, rep from * once more, 2dc, ch3, 2dc into last ch3sp, ch1, join with ss into ch3.
Row 3: ch3 (counts as 1dc), 1dc into each of next 4sts, * 2dc, ch3, 2dc into 1st ch3sp, 1dc into each of next 7sts, rep from * once more, 2dc, ch3, 2dc into last ch3sp, ch1, join with ss into tch.

Shawl triangle
Using yarn A, ch 4, join with ss. **Row 1:** ch4 (counts as 1dc and ch1), 3dc into ring, ch2, 3dc into ring, ch1, 1dc into ring, turn. **Row 2:** ch4 (counts as 1dc and ch1), 3dc into ch sp, ch1, (3dc, 2ch, 3dc) into corner ch3sp, ch1, 3dc into ch sp, ch1, 1dc into ch sp, turn. **Row 3:** ch4 (counts as 1dc and ch1), (3dc into next ch sp) twice, ch1, (3dc, 2ch, 3dc) into corner ch3sp, ch1, (3dc into ch sp) twice, ch1, 1dc into ch sp, join with ss into tch.

blizzard

Materials

size G hook

Sublime Baby Cashmere Merino Silk DK in Vanilla (A)

DMC Lumina in Silver (B)

Project notes

Christmas tree ornament. Before fastening off yarn, chain 10 and ss into the same stitch to form a chain loop. Use the loop to hang on the tree or as part of a garland.

Main pattern: using yarn A, ch6, join with ss to form a ring.

Round 1: ch3 (counts as 1dc), 15dc into ring, join with ss into ch3.

Round 2: ch5 (counts as 1dc and ch2), 1dc in base of 5ch, sk1, * (1dc, ch2, 1dc) into next st, sk1, rep from * 6 more times, join with ss into top of ch3.

Round 3: ss into 1st ch2sp, ch3 (counts as 1dc), 1dc, ch3, 2dc in same sp, * (2dc, ch3, 2dc) into next ch2sp, rep from * 6 more times, join with ss into top of ch3.

Round 4: ss into next 2sts and 1st ch2sp, * make picot (MP) as follows: (ch3, ss into 3rd ch from hook) 3 times, work 1sc into each of next 4sts, rep from * 7 times, ending last rep working 1sc into each of last 2sts.

Make loop by working ch10, ss into next st. Fasten off and weave in ends.

NOW TRY THIS

Sparkling snowflake

Work as given for main pattern in yarn B for a sparkly effect.

Large snowflake

Using yarn A, work Rounds 1–3 as given for main pattern. **Round 4:** ss into next ch3sp, ch3 (counts as 1dc), (2dc, ch3, 3dc) into chsp, *(3dc, ch3, 3dc) into next chsp**, repeat from * to ** around, join with ss to top of ch3. **Round 5:** ss into chsp. *make picot (MP) 5 times, ss into each of next 6 dc**, repeat from * to ** around, join with ss into ss at beg of round.

Flower center

Using yarn A, ch6, join with ss to form a ring. **Round 1:** (ch2, 1dc, ch2, ss to ring) to make petal, rep 5 times more. **Round 2:** ss into ch2 and dc, *ch12, ss into 9th ch from hook, ch3, sk next 4 ch, 1sc into next dc**, rep from * to **, ss into first ss made. **Round 3:** 3sc into 3chsp, (3sc, MP, 3sc) into 8ch lp, 3sc into 3chsp**, rep from * to ** 5 times more, join with ss into ss at beg of round.

flutterby

Materials

size G hook

King Cold Bamboo Cotton in Moss (A), Rose (B), Cobalt (C), Aqua (D), Purple (E)

Main pattern: using yarn B, ch4, join with ss to form a ring.

Round 1: ch4, 3dc into ring, ch3, ss into ring, ch3, 3dc into ring, ch4, ss into ring,* ch3, 3dc into ring, ch3, ss into ring, rep from * once more. Fasten off and weave in ends.

Using the picture as a guide, make the abdomen and antennae parts by sewing around the middle with yarn A.

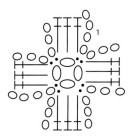

NOW TRY THIS

High flying
Using yarn C, ch4, join with ss to form a ring. **Round 1:** * ch2, 3dc into ring, ch2, ss into ring, rep from * 3 more times. Fasten off and finish as in main pattern.

In the air
Using yarn D, ch4, join with ss to form a ring. **Round 1:** * ch3, 3dc into ring, ch4, ss into ring, rep from * 3 times more. Fasten off and finish as in main pattern.

Featherweight
Using yarn E, ch4, join with ss to form a ring. **Round 1:** * ch4, 3dc into ring, ch4, ss into ring, rep from * once more, ** ch3, 2sc into ring, ch3, ss into ring, rep from ** once more to end. Fasten off and finish as in main pattern.

fall in love

Materials
size G hook: main, Picot edge leaf
size D hook: Maple leaf, Clover leaf
Debbie Bliss Cotton DK in Brown (A)
Rowan Cotton Glace in Dijon (B)
Persimmon (C)

Main pattern: using yarn A, ch10.
Round 1: 1dc into 3rd ch from hook, work (1dc, 1hdc, 1tr, 1dc, 1hdc, 1sc, 1sc) along ch, make picot as follows: (ch3, ss into 1st ch), then work back along the underside of chain as follows: (1sc, 1sc, 1hdc, 1dc, 1tr, 1hdc, 1dc). Fasten off, leaving short tail for stalk.

NOW TRY THIS

Picot edge leaf
Using yarn A, work as given for main leaf, do not fasten off yarn at the end of Round 1, work picot edge as follows:
Round 2: make 1st picot (MP) as follows: ch3, ss into 1st ch. Sk1, ss into next st, * MP, sk1, ss into next st, rep from * to end, ch4 for stalk.

Maple leaf
Using yarn C, ch4, join with ss to form ring.
Round 1: ch3 (counts as 1dc), 11dc into ring, join with ss into ch3. **Round 2:** ch3, 1dc into first st, 2dc into each of next 2sts, ch7, MP — ss into 3rd ch from hook, work into rem ch4 as follows (1sc, 1hdc, 2dc, 3tr around stem of dc), ss into next st, * ch8, MP — ss into 3rd ch from hook, work into rem ch4 as follows (1sc, 1hdc, 2dc, 3tr into last ch), sk1, ss into next st, rep from * 3 more times, work 2dc into each st to end, join with 1dc into ch3, ch4 for stalk. Fasten off.

Clover leaf
Using yarn B, ch5, join with ss to form ring. **Round 1:** * ch3, 2dc into ring, ch3, ss into ring, rep from * twice more, ch3 to make stalk.

85

kind hearts

Materials

size G hook

Debbie Bliss Cotton DK in
Red (A), Pale Green (B),
Mushroom (C), Pale Blue (D)

Project notes

Heart garland. Work 3 hearts in each color,
join using ch in contrasting color, 15ch
between each heart, and ss to top of each
heart to join.

Main pattern: using yarn D, ch3, join with ss to form a ring.

Round 1: ch3 (counts as 1dc), 11dc into ring, join with ss into tch.

Round 2: ch1, sk ch3 of prev round, 1sc into next st, work (1hdc, 1dc, 1hdc) into next st, 1sc into each of next 3sts, ch1, 1dc into next st, ch1, 1sc into each of next 3sts, work (1dc, 1hdc, 1dc) into next st, 1sc into last st, ss into ch3.

Round 3: ch1, 1sc into each of next 2sts, 3sc into next st, 1sc into each of next 4sts, 2sc into next chsp, 3sc into next st, 2sc into next ch sp, 1sc into each of next 4sts, 3sc into next st, 1sc into each of last 2sts, ch1, ss into ch1. Fasten off and weave in ends.

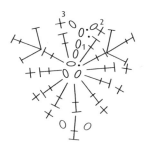

NOW TRY THIS

Contrast border

Work Rounds 1–2
as given for main
pattern in yarn A, and
Round 3 in yarn B.

Solid center heart

Use yarn C.

Row 1: ch7, 1hdc into 3rd ch from hook, 1hdc into each of next 4sts, turn. **Row 2:** ch2, 1hdc into each st to end. Repeat row 2 once more. **Row 3:** sk1, 7tr into next st, ch2, ss into next st, ch2, 7tr into next st, ss into top of tr.

Loop center heart

Using yarn B, ch4, join with ss to form a ring.

Round 1: ch1 (counts as 1dc), 11sc into ring, join with ss into ch1. **Round 2:** *3sc into next st, 1sc into each of next 2sts**, rep from * to ** 3 times more. Join with ss. **Round 3:** 1sc into each of next 2sts, sk1, 7dc into next st, sk2, 1sc into next st, sk2, 7dc into next st, sk1, 1sc in next st.

big love

Materials

size G hook

Debbie Bliss Cotton DK in Pale Blue (A), Teal (B), Red (C), Mustard (D)

Main pattern: using yarn A, ch3, join with ss to form a ring.

Round 1: ch3 (counts as 1dc), 2dc into ring, * ch3, 3dc into ring, rep from * twice more, ch3, join with ss into tch.

Round 2: ss into next 3sts, ch3, (2dc, ch3, 2dc) into chsp, ch1, *(3dc, ch3, 3dc) into chsp, ch1**, rep from * to ** twice more, ss to ch3.

Round 3: ss into next 3sts, ch3, sk3, 7tr into next chsp, sk3, 1sc into next chsp, sk3, 7tr into next st, sk3, ss into next chsp, ss into each of next 3sts. Fasten off and weave in ends.

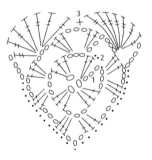

NOW TRY THIS

To and fro

Using yarn D, ch2.
Row 1: 2sc into 2nd ch from hook, turn. **Row 2:** ch1, 1sc into 1st st, 2sc into 2nd st, turn.
Row 3 (inc): ch1, 1sc into 1st st, 1sc into each st to last st, 2sc in last st, turn. Repeat last row until 19sts. Shape top as

follows. **Next row:** 1sc into 9sts, turn. **Next row (dec):** ch1, sk1, 1sc into each st to last 2sts, sk1, 1sc into last st, turn. Repeat last row until 2sts. Fasten off. Rejoin yarn to rem sts and repeat shape top, do not break off yarn. Work 1sc into each st and row around the outer edge of heart working 3sc into point.

Picot edge heart

Make a heart using the "to and fro" variation.

Using yarn C * ch3, ss into 3rd ch from hook, sk1, ss into next st, rep from * to end. Fasten off.

Lacy edge heart

Make a heart using the "to and fro" variation. Using yarn B, 1sc into 1st st, * ch3, sk2, 1sc into next st, rep from * to end.

cute crochet

Materials

size D hook

Any DK weight yarn in rainbow colors

key chain for project

Project notes:

Key chain or mobile. Using embroidery thread, attach a design to a key chain for a key ring. Alternatively, use all the emblems together to make a baby's mobile.

Main pattern: to make a rainbow, ch8 using violet yarn.

Row 1: 1sc into 2nd ch from hook, 1dc into next ch, 2dc into next ch, 1dc into next ch, 2dc into next ch, 1dc into next ch, 1sc into last ch, turn. Break off violet and join in indigo.

Row 2: ch1, 1sc into each of next 2sts, 2sc into next st, 1sc into each of next 3sts, 2sc into next st, 1sc into each st to end, turn. Break off indigo and join in blue.

Row 3: ch1, 1sc into 1st 2sts, * 2sc into next st, 1sc into each of next 2sts, rep from * to end, turn. Break off blue and join in green.

Row 4: work as Row 3. Break off green and join in yellow.

Row 5: ch1, 1sc into 1st 2sts, 2sc into next st, 1sc into each of next 3sts, 2sc into next st, 1sc into each of next 4sts, 2sc into next st, 1sc into each of next 3sts, 2sc into next st, 1sc into each st to end, turn. Break off yellow and join in orange.

Row 6: ch1, 1sc into 1st 2sts, 2sc into next st, 1sc into each of next 4sts, 2sc into next st, 1sc into each of next 6sts, 2sc into next st, 1sc into each of next 4sts, 2sc into next st, 1sc into each st to end, turn. Break off orange and join in red.

Row 7: ch1, 1sc into each of next 12sts, 2sc into each of next 2sts, 1sc into each st to end. Fasten off and weave in ends.

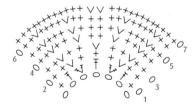

NOW TRY THIS

Crescent moon

Using yellow yarn, ch12. **Row 1:** 1sc into 2nd ch from hook, 1sc into next ch, 2dc into each of next ch7, 1sc into each ch to end, turn. **Row 2:** sk1 * 1sc into each of next 2sts, 2sc into next ch, rep from * to end, ss into last st.

Sun

Round 1: Using yellow yarn, ch2, 9hdc into 1st ch, join with ss into ch2. **Round 2:** ch2, 1hdc into 1st st, 2hdc into each st to end, join with ss into ch2. **Round 3:** as Round 2. **Round 4:** * ch7, ss into 3rd ch from hook, work back down into remaining 4ch as follows: 1hdc into 1st ch, 1dc into next ch,

1tr into each of last ch2, sk3, ss into next st of circle (1st point worked), ss into next st, rep from * ending last rep with ss into base of ch7.

Blue moon

Work as given for Crescent moon, using blue yarn.

galaxy

Materials

size G hook: main

size H hook: Twinkly granny star,
     Cluster center star, Cluster star

Rowan All Seasons Cotton in
Damson (A), Blush (B), Jacuzzi (C),
String (D)

Debbie Bliss Cotton DK (E) in 3 colors if
     desired

Project notes

Garland. String stars together to make a
festive garland. See page 86.

Main pattern: using yarn E, ch5, join with ss to form a ring.
Round 1: ch3 (counts as first dc), 2dc into ring, * ch3, 3dc into ring, rep from * 3
more times, ch3, join with ss into ch3. Change yarn color if desired.
Round 2: ss along and into 1st ch3sp, ch3 (counts as 1dc), (2dc, ch3, 3dc) into
same sp (1st corner worked), ch1, * (3dc, ch3, 3dc) into next ch3sp, ch1, rep from
* to end, join with ss into ch3. Change yarn color if desired.
Round 3: ss along and into next corner sp, ch3 (counts as 1dc), (2dc, ch4, 3dc)
into same sp (1st point worked), 1sc into next ch1sp, * (3dc, ch4, 3dc) into next
ch3sp, 1sc into next ch1sp, rep from * to end, join with ss into ch3. Fasten off and
weave in ends.

Twinkly granny star

Using yarn A, work
as given for main
pattern for Rounds 1–3.
Change to yarn B and
work edging as follows:
Round 4: ch1, 1sc into 1st 2sts, work (1sc,
make picot (MP) as follows: ch3, 1ss into
3rd ch from hook, 1sc) into 1st ch4sp, *
1sc into next 7sts, (1sc, MP, 1sc) into next
ch4sp, rep from * ending last rep with 1sc
into last st, join with ss into ch1.

Cluster center star

Using yarn C, ch6, join
with ss. **Round 1:** ch3,
2dc cl into ring. * ch2,
3dc cl into ring. Repeat
from * 6 more times. Ch2,
ss into ch3 to join. Ss along to ch sp.
Round 2: ch3 (counts as first dc), 2dc.
** ch1, 3dc into next ch sp. Repeat from
** around. Ch1, join with ss. **Round 3:** ch3
(counts as first dc), 2dc, ch4, 3dc into ch sp.
Into each ch sp work (3dc, ch4, 3dc). Join
with ss.

Cluster star

Using yarn D, work
Round 1 as for the
cluster center star.
Round 2: ch3, 3dc cl
into ch sp. * ch3, 4dc
cl into ch sp. Repeat from * around. Ch3,
join with ss. Ss along to next ch sp.
Round 3: ch3 (counts as first dc), 3dc cl,
ch5, 4dc cl into next ch sp, * 4dc cl, ch5, 4dc
cl into each ch sp. Repeat from * around.
Join with ss. Fasten off.

index